ILLUSTRATED

DICTIONARY

of BIBLE MANNERS

and CUSTOMS

ILLUSTRATED
DICTIONARY

of BIBLE
MANNERS
and CUSTOMS

By
DR. A. VAN DEURSEN

Illustrated by
J. DE VRIES   PHILOSOPHICAL LIBRARY, INC.

Published, 1967, by
Philosophical Library, Inc.,
15 East 40th Street, New York 16, N.Y.

ISBN 0-8065-0707-1

Distributed to the trade by
CITADEL PRESS
A division of Lyle Stuart, Inc.
120 Enterprise Ave., Secaucus, N.J. 07094

CONTENTS

CONTENTS

INTRODUCTION

Wherever we turn in the Bible we shall almost certainly find references to objects familiar in the Middle East in ancient times. Towns have their walls and gates, agriculture has its threshing instruments and carts, large houses have their corner-stones and courtyards, the tabernacle has its altars and lavers of brass—and so forth. We often wonder how we are to picture these things. What did a barber's razor look like? What are walls and bulwarks? What is the meaning of the word "pit" in the Authorised Version? A clearer picture of these everyday objects will help towards a better understanding of the Bible.

There are books and publications that could be consulted, but not everyone has the time or the opportunity to do so. Hence this volume, giving a classified collection of illustrations of various terms, objects, manners and customs in the Bible. As a rule the drawings are based on data provided by archaeological research, primarily by excavations; no attempt has been made to give any hypothetical reconstructions. The scope is thereby restricted to those subjects on which adequate information is available.

In order to give a more vivid sense of direct contact with the past frequent quotations are made from ancient sources. I have visited many of the sites mentioned and studied many of the objects in the museums of Cairo, Paris, Rome and Tel Aviv, being particularly indebted to the Library Ex Oriente Lux at Leiden and the Bibliotheca Rosenthalia at Amsterdam.

A number of additional terms, selected in consultation with Dr. H. Bergema, have been added to this edition.

A. VAN DEURSEN

1. THE CITY AND ITS WALLS

1. Tell el-Hesy, a mound after partial levelling. Where once an ancient city stood, a heap of ruins is all that is now left. In the Authorized Version such a mound is called a "heap". Joshua "made Ai an heap" (Joshua 8: 28) and Jeremiah says of Jerusalem that the city will be rebuilt "on her own heap", on the mound (Jer. 30: 18).

2. Section of Tell el-Hesy, where archaeologists have been able to establish the existence of eight cities of various periods corresponding to successive layers in the soil. The figures on the left give the height in feet. It is possible to deduce the age of a settlement from remnants of their civilization and to date a layer by studying broken fragments of pottery. The archaeologist Bliss found in the fourth city a clay tablet which obviously belonged to the same category as the El Amarna letters and could hence be given a date in the fifteenth century. Scarabs of the eighteenth dynasty (signets giving the imprint of a dung-beetle, a prominent symbol in Egyptian religion) also indicated that a likely date would be somewhere near 1400 B.C., which gives us a reasonably accurate date for the fourth city, immediately above the ash stratum (*aa*). Perhaps Tell el-Hesy corresponds to Eglon in Joshua 10: 3.

3. Wall of Tell Beit Mirsim (the ancient Kiriath-sepher, "the city of books", taken by Othniel, Judges 1: 12). In those days city walls were of a composite structure consisting of a rampart of sand and rubble with a facing of heavy stone blocks on the outside (*a*). The inside may have a second wall to hold the earth and rubble in place.

The figure standing at the foot of the wall gives some idea of its height, which would account for the Scouts' anxiety: the cities are great and walled up to heaven (Deut. 1: 28).

4. Gate flanked by towers. In general there was only one gate in the wall of the smaller cities ("the gate of the city", Luke 7: 12). The doors themselves (*d*) were reinforced with iron (Isa. 45: 2). On each side of the gate there were towers (*a*) which, according to Professor de Groot, were perhaps twelve metres wide, jutting out some distance, and surrounded by a continuous row of battlements for defence purposes. Above the gate (*c*) was the place for the watchman (2 Sam. 18: 24).

5. Double walls. Some cities, of which Jericho was one, were surrounded by double walls. The inner wall (*c*) had a thickness of 3·3–3·7 metres and was surrounded by an apron wall (*a*), 1·5–1·6 metres thick. This outer wall is sometimes called a bulwark in the Authorized Version (Isa. 26: 1). Jeremiah grieved over Zion: He made the rampart (*a*) and the wall (*c*) to lament (Lam. 2: 8). The walls were built of mud bricks on a foundation of rocks from the fields. At one corner of the inner wall stood a strong tower or fortress (*b*), the last point of defence (Judges 9: 49, 51). Between the gate of the outer wall (*b*) and of the inner wall (*e*) was the space between the two gates (2 Sam. 18: 24). The gate is near the well (*g*); it was of course of vital importance that the city should have water, and so it was built near a well (cf. Rama, 1 Sam. 9: 11). The projections (*c*) served as archers' positions.

8

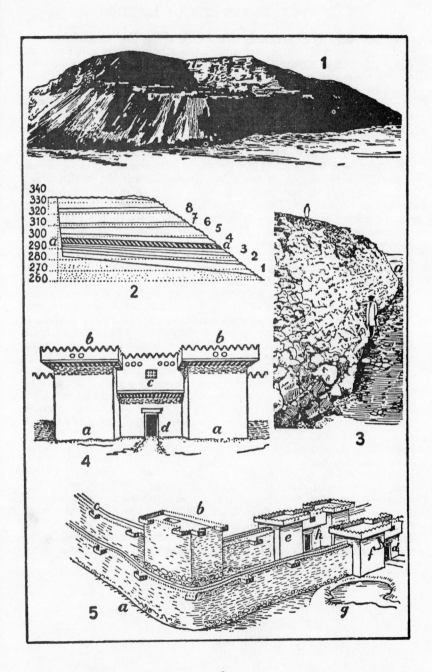

2. VIEW OF THE CITY OF MEGIDDO

View of the city of Megiddo at the time of the first kings (about the tenth century B.C. in the opinion of the scholars who excavated the mound of Tell el-Mutesellim). They gave the name "the large house" to the extensive building (*ac*) which stood near the north-east wall. This large house, which is attributed to the tenth century B.C. because of the stratum in which it was discovered, was presumably the head-quarters of the commandant or possibly the residence of the governor, Baana (1 Kings 4: 12). Next to this building was a paved courtyard (*b*) where the soldiers used to assemble before climbing the steps to the city wall (*g*). Near the steps was also the commandant's watch-tower (*c*). This tower was built of cut and levelled freestone. Typical of their method, also apparent in the outer city wall, was the position of a bondstone next to two stretchers, with a course of stretchers in the next layer. The wall of the large house also consisted of cut stones—three rows of hewed stones (1 Kings 7: 12; see also 3, 1), built on a foundation of rough stone (*f*) and braced with cedar beams (*e*). The presence of this wood could be deduced from ash found in the inner court, from which it was clear that the beams had fallen victim to flames that had left the masonry almost unscathed. The upright beams (*e*) carried the joists of the ceiling (*d*). The "Large House" in Megiddo is reminiscent of Solomon's palace: and a great court round about was with three rows of hewed stones, and a row of cedar beams (1 Kings 7: 12). Informed opinion compares the architectural style of Megiddo with Solomon's at Jerusalem on the one hand, and with the Hittites' on the other. This house in Megiddo also bears some resemblance to Ahab's palace in Samaria. Both in its execution and its design it is manifestly the work of accomplished craftsmen. The foundations reveal a rare feature—horizontal beams forming a plate. To the left of the building is the great, massive city wall; the top of the wall is wide enough to accommodate both the guards and a defending army. The view from the walls across the city gives an impression of flat roofs at about the same height, intersected by the narrow streets running between the houses. In the street in front of the large house is a chariot drawn by two horses. It was at Megiddo that the famous stables of Solomon were found. Megiddo was a fortress: one of the chariot cities and "the cities of the horsemen" (2 Chron. 8: 6; 1 Kings 9: 17–19); a fortress in a key position at the entrance to the famous valley of Megiddo. Many battles have been fought in that valley; the word Armageddon (Rev. 16: 16) is sometimes rendered by "Mount Megiddo". This accounts for the title "New Light from Armageddon" given by the director of operations to his book recording these discoveries.

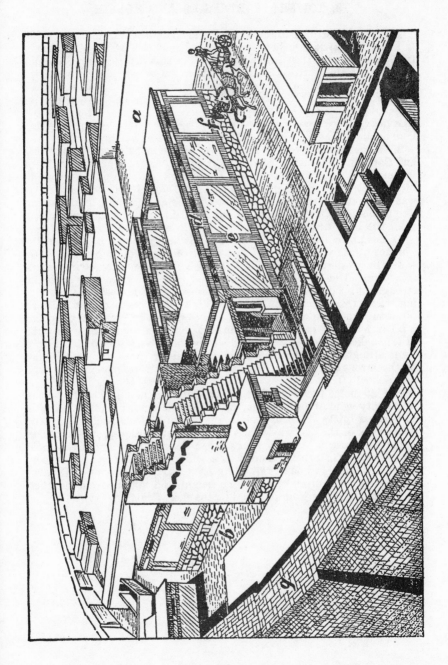

3. TOWERS, FORTRESSES AND HOUSES

1. Israelite fortified tower in Samaria. Samaria was built on a hill (1 Kings 16: 24) at "the head of the fat valleys" (Isa. 28: 1). Completely isolated as it was, the place was admirably suited for defence. Condor claims that this fortress must have been impregnable before the invention of gunpowder. Its defences consisted of walls and towers or citadels. Typical of the post-Solomonian style was this stacking of large oblong stone blocks (*a*) ground smooth on the outer face (*b*). The heavy, accurately shaped stones fit neatly on top of one another; here again "three rows of hewed stones". (See 2, l. 15.)

2. Reconstruction of the fortress of Shechem between Mount Ebal and Gerizim. The city of Shechem (*c*), unlike most of the other cities of Palestine, was not built on the top of a natural hill, but at the widening of the valley between Gerizim (*a*) and Ebal (*b*). The oldest settlement was situated on a terrace on the almost flat spur of Mount Ebal, looking like a shoulder (for that is what the word Shechem means) projecting from the head of the mountain (Professor Böhl).

This is probably where "the hold (*c*) of the house of the God Berith" (Judges 9: 46) was excavated, the tower of Shechem with its bulwark.

3. The western stronghold at Taanach (Professor Thiersch's reconstruction). The wall in the background is the city wall (*a*) with the stronghold inside it. This citadel (*bb*) was a large, almost square building, 20 x 21·8 metres. The courtyard (*c*) to the right had in it a cistern (*d*), a sunken basin which the A.V. calls a cistern in Proverbs 5: 15 and a pit in Matthew 12: 11. The court was enclosed by rooms with walls of soft-baked bricks (*e*), reinforced with wooden beams. A flight of steps leads straight from the courtyard to the upper floor and to the roof of the stronghold. This then was where the watchman on the wall was posted (*f*).

4. Flat-roofed houses inside the city wall. The majority of the houses in the city would be small, four-walled, single-story buildings made of soft-baked bricks (*c*) on a foundation of stone blocks and rocks. The framework of the doorway consisted of two stone side-posts (*d*) and an upper door-post (*e*) as they are called in Exodus 12: 7 and a threshold (*f*) (1 Kings 14: 17). If there was a window at all, one (*g*) was considered enough (Joshua 2: 18). Steps (*a*) led to the flat roof (*b*). Because the houses were often of the same height and adjoined one another, it was easy to pass from one roof to the next (Matt. 24: 17).

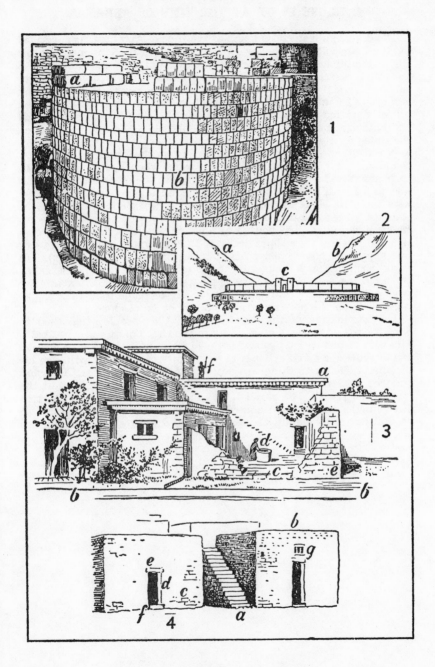

4. HOUSE IN UR AT THE TIME OF ABRAHAM

The drawing illustrates a house at the time of Abraham, as envisaged by the archaeologist Woolley as a result of excavations made at the site of the biblical Ur. These houses, built after 2100 and destroyed in 1885 B.C., reveal that Abraham and his ancestors in Ur lived in a city with a high standard of civilisation; the houses testify to comfort and luxury. The inhabitants of Ur lived in houses built of soft-baked bricks rendered in plaster and whitewash. The rooms surrounded an inner courtyard from which they derived light and air; for on the outside only blank, windowless walls faced the narrow, crooked, unpaved streets. The front door led from the street to the ante-chamber (*v*) containing a gutter full of water where visitors could wash their hands and feet and from here proceed to the inner court (*b*). This was paved with bricks (*a,a*) and in Babylon the joints were often filled with bitumen, slime in the A.V. (Gen. 11: 3). In one corner was the staircase (*c*) leading to the gallery (*e*), which gave access to the rooms on the upper floor. The house was finished off with a flat roof (*f*), constructed to allow for a slight declivity from the inner edge. The gallery was supported on wooden posts (*p*) with or without plinths (*n*). (In Israel too, the large houses of the elite also had such posts, called beams in the A.V. (Hab. 2: 11) or pillars (Prov. 9: 1)). There are two large pots (*d*) on the courtyard floor which, to judge from their shape, were made on the potter's wheel and not by hand alone.

An examination of the floors revealed that people often used to bury their dead under a mud casing in the shape of an upturned bath. This custom of burying the dead in the house or in the yard has a parallel in 1 Samuel 25: 1 and 1 Kings 2: 34. Professor de Groot writes in his account: "The same thing was noted in the excavations at Gezer and Jericho; at Gezer during the Canaanite period, in Jericho even at the time of the Jews." The burial of men in upturned baths, or of children in jars under the floors of houses, burial in dolmens, in tumuli and in natural caves, all signify the same general ideas regarding the future life.

5. HOUSES

1. Larger houses in an Eastern city. It was noticed at various sites that there was a considerable difference between the inside partition walls (between the several rooms) and the more solid outside walls. Sellin and Watzinga found in Jericho a house of five rooms grouped round an inner court and Macalister found a house of the later Greek period at Gezer with twelve rooms. In such houses the door (a) gave access to a room which led to the inner court (b), referred to in the A.V. simply as the court (Neh. 8: 16). A gallery built on posts or pillars surrounded the court. The steps (d) led up to the flat roof which was enclosed by a parapet (f), called a battlement in the A.V. (Deut. 22: 8). The house on the left has in addition an upper-room (h) on the roof; in the story of Ehud it is called a summer parlour (Judges 3: 20). It was indeed not uncommon even for smaller houses to have such upper rooms (1 Kings 17: 19). The finest houses would have a latticed window (g) in the women's room (cf. Judges 5: 28). At the time of building, the corner-stones (e) were dressed and set in place with the utmost care so as to make them the headstones of the corners (Ps. 118: 22).

2. A village home in Palestine. The farmhouses in Palestine consisted as a rule of one room only. All lived happily together on the hard mud floor (2 Sam. 12: 3), except for the fact that the animal quarter (b) was on a slightly lower level; a few rough steps in the middle led up to the raised part (a) where the people themselves lived. On either side of the steps were fodder troughs or cribs (c), so well known to the ox (d) and ass (e), as Isaiah 1: 3 tells us. To the right is a goat (f), kept for its milk (Prov. 27: 27). In the middle of the raised part of the house is a round loam ring, 4 inches high, inside which the fire glows (g), and at night all sleep on the floor with their feet towards this loam ring. Hence the objection to getting up at night to lend three loaves to a friend (Luke 11: 7), for with this sleeping arrangement there was always the risk of treading on the others and waking up the family. The woman is sitting at her hand-mill (h). The child lying in the hammock is wrapped in swaddling clothes (i) (Ezek. 16: 4).

3. Tool made of lava for smoothing down plaster on walls. (Found in the excavation at Teleilat Ghassûl in the Jordan Valley). The walls of a house "were plastered with mud and chalk" ("the one built up a wall and others daubed it with untempered mortar", Ezek. 13: 10).

6. MEALS

1. Assyrian meal. A number of men are seated round a large pot (*a*); one of them, on the right, ladles out the broth with a cup (*c*), which would then be handed round. For solid food they used their fingers, as eastern people do to this day. The Assyrians' main meals were in the morning and in the evening. In the mansions of the wealthy the master of the house would call out to his servants: Bring me water (*b*), pour it over my hands, I wish to dine. The hungry ones smacked their lips to express their appetite and reached eagerly for the food brought by the servants. After the meal they wiped their faces with a towel and the servants poured water over their hands. Small dogs kept in the house walked round the room eating "the crumbs from their masters' table".

2. Egyptian Meal. The man to the left of the table spread with food (*a*) is holding a tray of figs. The third man, at (*b*), is dealing with a goose, while the man on the right is holding a piece of meat. The Egyptian in (*c*) has in his hands a fish which he is going to eat; his companion opposite is drinking from a jug. There is another man eating fish on the left of (*d*), where the table, as in (*a*), has two baskets of grapes under it. The tables are clearly loaded with food, but forks are conspicuous by their absence; hands and fingers are used instead. They are sitting on the floor, as chairs were never used at their meals.

3. Banquet (a Phoenician carving found in Cyprus). Three adults are reclining at table, the left arm supported by the arm of the couch. Two of them are men wearing pointed, cone-shaped hats (*a*, *b*). They have short beards but a smooth upper lip, and are wearing long mantles. The third figure (*c*) is a woman, wearing a head-cloth round her cheeks and chin. The man on the right (*a*) has on his knee a child wrapped in a long gown; a girl, judging from her round cap.

The custom of sitting at table in ancient times is recorded in Judges 19: 6, 1 Samuel 20: 5 and notably in 1 Kings 13: 20. When someone wished to pay his guests special honour, he did not join them at the meal but stood serving them at table (Gen. 18: 8). There is a possible reference to reclining at table in Amos 6: 4. Also, the word "lay" for the Authorized Version's "sat" is used by Moffatt in Matthew 26: 7 and Mark 14: 3.

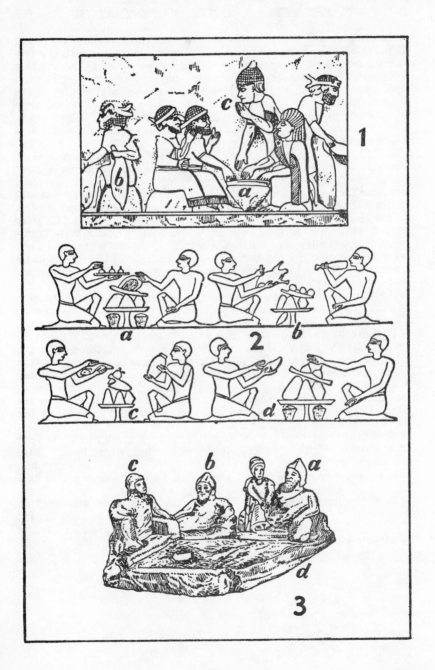

19

7. THE TENT ; ARTICLES IN EVERYDAY USE

1. Tent. A tent was generally erected with three sets of three poles; the longest poles were set up in a line down the centre with the two shorter sets of poles on either side, and all were tied to one another with ropes. The canvas or fabric was stretched tightly over the top and made fast with "cords" (b) (Jer. 10: 20) to "stakes" (a) in the ground (Isa. 54: 2). These stakes, made of very hard wood, were about two feet long and were hammered into the ground (Judges 4: 21). The tent was covered with cloths woven from goat's hair, which was black (Song of Sol. 4: 1; 1: 5).

2. Lamp. So many small earthen lamps have been unearthed at excavations, especially from graves, that it is possible to trace their development from the rough and ready open-dish type to the more practical form of oil lamp with sharply tapering spout, which was still in use during the Israelite period, and the more or less enclosed models of the Hellenistic period. An illustration is given of a lamp of a later period, which one can safely assume was still being used in New Testament times. In the story of 2 Samuel 21: 17, David's friends do not want him to go out again to battle, for "the light of Israel" might be quenched. This light of Israel is the King, the symbol of prosperity and life for the people (cf. Ps. 132: 17). It is generally thought that a lamp was kept alight all night in every house in Israel (on the strength of Proverbs 31: 18—her candle goeth not out by night.) The expression "his candle shall be put out" (Job 18: 6) refers to death and destruction.

3. Stove at Taanach. The object illustrated was first thought to be an altar of incense. It is in the form of a pyramid, three feet high, with holes in the four sides, probably intended as draft intakes. It is made of baked clay. The sides are decorated with lions and sphinxes, a sacred tree and the figure of a man holding a snake. Such a hearth or stove was what king Jehoiakim sat near. (Jeremiah 36: 22. Now the king sat in the winterhouse in the ninth month: and there was a fire on the hearth burning before him.)

4. Earthenware cruses for olive oil, in which a stock of oil was kept in the house. They were kept in a special place where it was dark, since light and air turned the oil rancid; for this reason the cruses had a comparatively narrow neck. Vials of oil are mentioned in 1 Samuel 10: 1; 2 Kings 9: 1; oil in a cruse 1 Kings 17: 12.

5. Earthenware waterpots. Pitchers like these were also used in ancient times. (John 2: 6; 1 Sam. 26: 11; 1 Kings 19: 6; Gen. 24: 16; Judges 7: 16). A little water in a vessel (1 Kings 17: 10), an handful of meal in a barrel (1 Kings 17: 12).

8. POTTERY

1. **Large jar, without ear or neck,** found at Jericho (pre-Israelite-period up to about 1600 B.C.).

2. **Large jar with ear and handle;** at Jericho; pre-Israelite. Typical is the handle (a) projecting horizontally from the side of the vessel like a pucker in cloth, with indentations for the fingers. The original purpose of the handle was to facilitate the balancing of the jar on the head.

3. **Small jugs with handles;** Megiddo; pre-Israelite.

4. **Finely modelled egg-shaped jug;** Jericho; early Israelite; sixteenth–ninth century B.C.

5. **Philistine jug at Gezer,** a strapped pot with a decoration of birds painted in red and black on a white background.

6. **Vase with rings on neck and belly** (at Taanach; late Israelite period; ninth–sixth century B.C.

7. **Pitcher from Tel-Zakarye** (perhaps the Azekah of the Bible). Early Israelite. This jar and the one from Jericho are evidence of the heights of perfection attained by the potter's art, though we must make allowances for foreign influences and even perhaps imports.

It has been found that pottery changes in form throughout the centuries, so that when, during excavations, fragments of pottery are found, it is possible to establish their age. Since the date of a settlement in a mound can be traced through these potsherds, a knowledge of ceramics is a prerequisite in all archaeological research. It is obvious, however, that fragments of earthenware vessels are only of value if they show one or other of the characteristic features of their period (handle, shape of the belly, rim and decoration).

Potter's vessels were very brittle. It would often happen that "the pitcher be broken at the fountain" (Eccles. 12: 6). The fragments also had their practical use, for, in order to make cisterns and pits watertight, they were covered with a cement made from chalk and ash which, in its turn, was covered with potsherds in order to obtain a rough surface, and when this was dry it was plastered over with a mixture of chalk and finely ground shards. Moreover, the potter added to his clay a grit made by pulverizing these fragments in order to make sure of its setting. With this in view, all the potsherds in a district were collected and ground down under a round stone. Psalm 2: 9, "Thou shalt dash them in pieces like a potter's vessel" refers to this grinding of the broken pottery. Again in Isaiah 30: 14—"And he shall break it as the breaking of the potter's vessel that is broken in pieces". Cf. also Jeremiah 19: 11.

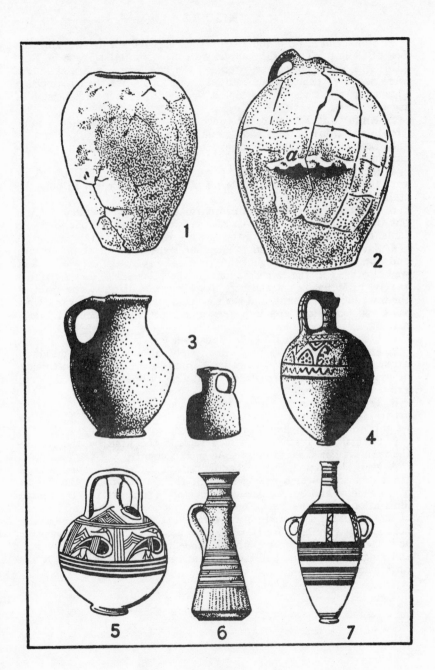

9. TOOLS

1. Stone knives (*a*, *b* and *c*) from Tell el-'Oreimeh (overlooking the Sea of Galilee). These flint knives date from the later Stone or Neolithic Age, which, of course, preceded the Iron Age. Such flint knives were used by Joshua when he used sharp knives for the circumcision (Joshua 5: 3). Zipporah too took a sharp stone for the circumcision of her son (Exod. 4: 25).

2. Knife. In the course of time, man has used knives of stone, bronze and iron; handles were made of wood or horn.

3. Lancet (as used by the priests of Baal for their self-inflicted torture in 1 Kings 18: 28).

4. Sickle. The sickle was used to cut the standing corn (Deut. 16: 9) with the right hand, while the left was used by the reaper to hold the stalks (Ps. 129: 7; Isa. 17: 5).

5. Hammer. Hammers were often made of chipped stone; cutting out the opening for the handle required a great deal of patience. In Israel the hammer was one of the smith's tools (Isa. 44: 12).

6. Saw. Saws have been found that were made of stone, ·bronze and iron. The saw was "shaken" (Isa. 10: 15) by the carpenter, and was also used in the forced labour at the brick kilns, *viz*: 2 Samuel 12: 31, in Moffatt's translation: "He also brought away the spoil of the town, a vast amount, and the townsfolk, whom he set to work with saws and iron picks and iron axes and made them labour at brickmaking."

(2–6 are taken from R. A. S. Macalister.)

7. Stone weights (from a photograph by Professor Böhl) found in excavations at Tell Beit Mirsim (i.e. Kiriath-sefer). Honesty in the use of weighing stones was required by divine ordinance (Deut. 25: 13; Prov. 16: 11).

8. Weighing of gold rings on scales as depicted by an Egyptian artist. On the right the rings (*a*), on the left the weights (*b*). These weights were in the shapes of animals (*c*).

9. Sundial, an instrument which records the time by the sun in the same way as those familiar to us in this country.

A vertical gnomon cast a shadow onto a surface engraved with a graduated scale which measured both the direction and the length of the shadow and by this means indicated the time of day. The centre illustration (*a*) shows the hole for the gnomon, (*b*) to the right, part of the graduated scale and (*c*) a decoration containing the figure of the falcon-headed godhead Re-Harmachis in a boat and holding a sceptre; he is facing Pharaoh Merenptah in a kneeling position. Above the god and king there is a sundial with adders; to the right and left of it are rings bearing the king's names.

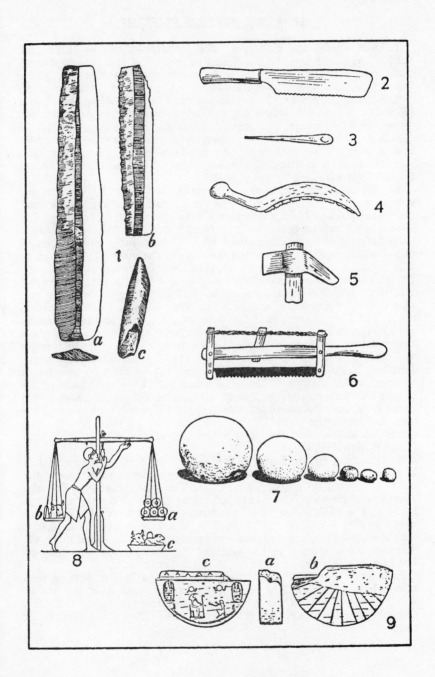

25

10. SAWS, SPADES, PLOUGHS

1. Saws, spades and pick-axes. The preparation of new ground for cultivation might involve the felling of trees and the hacking out of their roots (Joshua 17: 15, 18) and the removal of stones (Isa. 5: 2). Saws (*a*), spades (*b*) and pick-axes (*c*) were the tools used for this work.

2. Babylonian plough. Two humped oxen (*a*) are pulling the plough (*b*) which is driven by three men. The principal figure, probably the owner, in a long outer garment (*c*) holds the two plough-tails (*d*) in his hands. The labourers, being slaves, wear garments that come down to the knees. One of them (*e*), his hands raised, is driving the oxen on; the other (*f*) is dropping the seed from a bag into the seed funnel (*g*), which is attached to the plough.

3. Palestinian plough, used for tilling the soil ready for the summer corn in the plain of Esdraelon. The ploughman is holding the ox goad (*a*) in his right hand and is driving the animals on with it (Judges 3: 31). In his left hand he is holding the plough tail (*b*) which, at its lower extremity (in the ground) has a point (*c*) comparable with the share of a modern plough. In between the oxen is the yoke (*d*); attached to it is the plough-beam (*e*) with a wooden fork (*f*) fixed to it to hold the plough-tail at the required obtuse angle. The modern plough cuts the soil partly with the coulter and partly with the ploughshare which also lifts it from underneath, enabling the large concave blade to turn it over. The strip of earth thus lifted out of the furrow and turned lands next to the furrow. The Eastern plough, with its broad point, made a better job of breaking up the soil than of turning it over, so furrows and clods (*g*) were much smaller (Ps. 65: 11). The plough of the ancient Israelites had a metal ploughshare (1 Sam. 13: 20, 21), and was drawn by oxen (1 Kings 19: 19). The ploughman must have the handle of the plough-tail firmly in his grip in order to steer the plough; and would avoid rocks and bushes which would prove too much for the primitive construction of the plough and would break it. So there is a twofold reason to look ahead, and it is a bad ploughman who looks behind (Luke 9: 62).

4. Ploughing in an Egyptian drawing. I. A farm labourer with a kind of hoe or pick (*a*), a wooden tool in the shape of an A; one of the arms is tapered to a sharp point. II. The ploughman, holding the plough-tails (*b*) with both hands. III. The driver (*c*) driving the long-horned oxen. IV. A barrel (*d*) containing the seed. V. An Egyptian wearing a loin-cloth (*e*) like the others, standing in the characteristic attitude with arms across the chest and hands on the shoulders. VI. Another ploughman (*f*). The ancient Egyptians were obviously as keen on talking at their work as are their descendants.

5. Sowing (Egyptian drawing). I. Egyptian, kneeling, putting seed into a basket (*a*). II. The sower (*b*) takes the seed from the basket and scatters it behind the ploughman over the ploughed land. III. Oxen before the plough (*c*), the "young calf" (*d*) frisking in front of them.

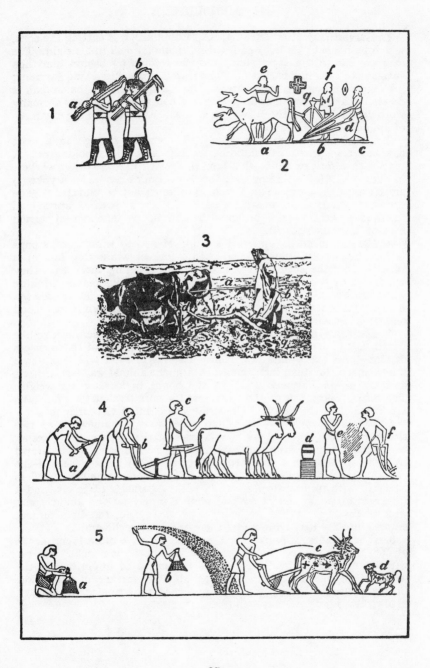

11. AGRICULTURE

1. Harvest (Egyptian drawing). An Egyptian (*a*) is cutting the corn, which he holds in his left hand, with a sickle (*b*) held in his right. The ears are cut with a short stem, and the woman (*c*) behind him then gathers the corn in a basket (*d*). The man is dressed in a long garment; his high standing is also apparent from his trim beard; the woman is dressed in a tunic and mantle (which is of course not what was normally worn during harvest; the drawing is an idealized fantasy of the dreamed-of abundance in the after-life).

2. Threshing (Egyptian drawing). The owner, dressed in a skirt covering his knees (*a*) is standing leaning on a stick, looking on. A man with a fork or winnowing fan (*c*), dressed like the other workers in a loin-cloth (*d*) is turning over the corn. Four oxen under a yoke (*e*) are treading the corn. (The threshing ox must not be muzzled !) The driver (*f*) goads them on with a stick. A servant with an apron tied like a pair of shorts (*g*) is bringing the corn in two hampers (*h*) carried here on a saddled ass (*i*).

3. Harvest scene (Egyptian drawing). Men with winnowers' scoops (*a*) are tossing the grain. A lad with a fork or winnowing fan (*b*) is turning over the corn. Three oxen (*c*) are treading the corn. They are driven by the driver (*d*) with a whip (*e*). A kneeling man is drinking water from a skin bottle (*f*) hanging in a sycamore or wild fig tree (*g*). A scribe (*h*) is noting down the number of measures of corn (*i*); a second one (*j*) is checking them for the granary accounts.

4. Threshing board. This consisted of a heavy, wooden, sledge-like board, the underside of which was covered with rows of sharp pieces of stone or metal points (*a*). Hence Isaiah 41: 15, I will make thee a new sharp threshing instrument. A draught animal was put in front and the *fellah* (farmer) stood on the board to increase its weight. The board was pulled to and fro across the corn so that the grain was separated from the ears and the straw was reduced to coarse chaff.

5. Threshing roller. A threshing roller had a framework of two sledge runners (*a*) joined by two laterals; a seat (*b*) for the thresher was constructed of posts and bars fixed to the runners. It was drawn by horse or mule on a rope attached to the front cross-piece and the two runners. In between these runners there were a number of rollers (*c*) faced with iron or steel discs (*d*), with a diameter of 32 cm. and a thickness of 3 mm., and they had teeth 8 mm. long and about 1 cm. wide at the base. When the implement was pulled, the discs turned, cutting into the ears lying under them and freeing the grain.

6. Wheat and cockle. Among the wheat (*a*) were often found heads of cockle (*b*). The people of Palestine imagined that cockle was bewitched wheat. In fact, cockle was the result of impurities in the wheat seed, and of course, propagated itself further in the fields. Cockle is alluded to in Job 31: 40, and the "tares among the wheat" in Matthew 13: 25, 28 may well refer to it also.

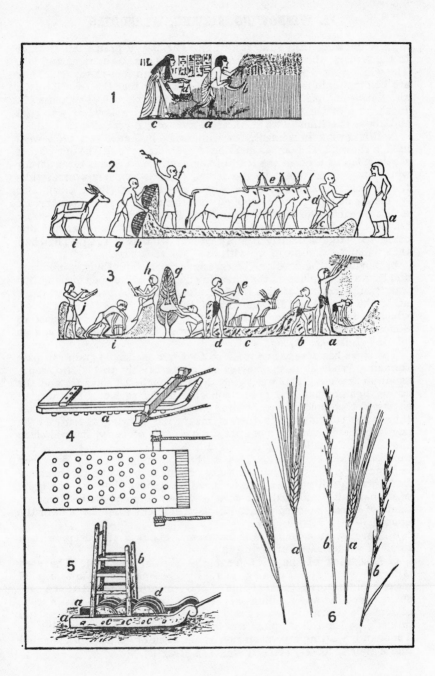

12. WINNOWING, SIEVING, MEASURING

1. Winnowing (Egyptian drawing). The heavy grains fall straight to the ground; the chaff (a) is scattered in an arc to the right and left. The winnowing women wear head-cloths (b) and loin-cloths (c). They are holding winnowing scoops with which they toss the corn into the air. One woman is sweeping up the grains with a brush of switches (d). In the top of the picture is a harvest sacrifice: a bowl of water (e) and above it a frame with the first sheaves of the year tied to it (f).

2. Winnowing implement. In winnowing in Israel two tools were used, a shovel, and a fan, as mentioned in Isaiah 30: 24. The illustration shows a fan as used in the land of Gennesareth. Wind is essential for winnowing; it must not be too strong (Jer. 4: 11), but a breeze like that which still blows in the morning and evening (Ruth 3: 2). For by means of the scoop (or shovel) and the fan, the grain was thrown into the wind, the heavier grains fell straight down and the straw fell by the side of the threshing-floor; if there was a strong wind one could see "the chaff driven away by the wind (Ps. 1: 4). The chaff that remained was burnt up with fire" (Matt. 3: 21).

3. Sieving of the corn on the threshing floor. Threshing, winnowing and sieving took place on the threshing floor (a) in the open air, and this was feasible enough after a rainless summer. Amos is an early writer using the metaphor "like as corn is sifted in a sieve" (Amos 9: 9), which is so well known in the searching words spoken by Christ to Simon: "Satan hath desired to have you, that he may sift you as wheat" (Luke 22: 31).

The sieve has a very fine mesh so that not one single grain can pass through. When it is shaken several times briskly to and fro, sand, small stones, chaff and weed seed drop through the sieve (b) and the straw, lighter than the grain, collects on the surface. The woman sifting (c) then holds the sieve tilted slightly away from her and adroitly throws the contents up in the air, meanwhile blowing as hard as she can into the descending mass. If she does this properly, she will clean the corn without losing a single grain and so completely that no impurities whatever remain. This is the operation partially described in Amos 9: 9: "For I will issue my command to shake the house of Israel among all nations, like corn within a sieve, but not one grain of it shall fall" (Moffatt). There is a wall or *jedar* in the background, made of loosely stacked stones (d), very different from the wall of the house (e).

4. Sieve, with a round wooden frame, about 8 cm. deep, with a mesh of woven sheep or goat gut.

5. Measuring of the corn (near the biblical Beeroth). The corn is measured on the threshing floor. By pressing and shaking a good measure is ensured (Luke 6: 38: "good measure pressed down and shaken together and running over"). The "measurer" (a) has in front of him the measuring barrel or measure (b). In order to do his job properly he has rolled up the sleeves of his cloak or outer garment (c). The man is wearing a kerchief tied at the back of his head (d). Behind him a wall of loosely stacked stones, a *jedar* (e).

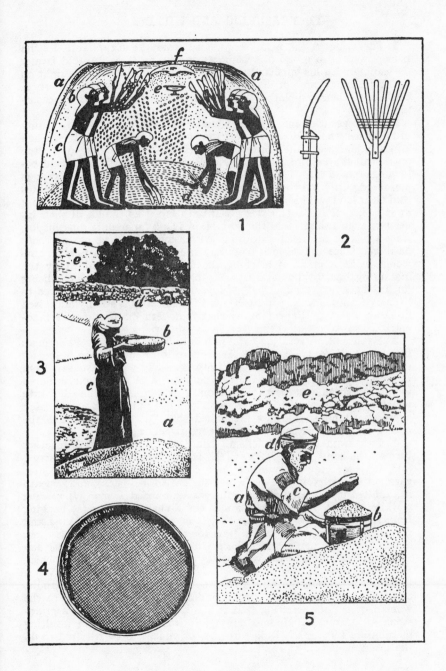

13. MEASURING AND MILLING

1. Surveying in the field (reproduced from the Egyptian). In the background (a) a group of sycamores or wild fig trees. An old farmer (b) leaning with his left hand on a naked boy (c) and with his right on a staff (d) is in charge of the party. Two men (e, f) are wearing shirts in addition to their loin-cloths. The field is being measured with a measuring line (g).

2. The measuring line and the boundary stones. Every village family in Palestine was entitled to a plot that fell to it by drawing lots. Such a plot of land was called *chelkah* in the Hebrew, e.g. 2 Kings 9: 25, the portion of the field of Naboth, or in Ruth 2: 3 a part of the field belonging unto Boaz. The plot to be allotted to a farmer for a year is measured with a measuring line (a). Amos warns the godless Israelites that their land will be divided by line and given to others; in Psalm 105: 11 it is said that Canaan was given unto Israel as the lot of their inheritance; in Psalm 16: 6 the poet praises God for maintaining his lot, since the lines are fallen unto him in pleasant places; he has a goodly heritage. Once the various plots had been allocated, the new tenants would make a point of marking the boundaries, determined by the measuring line, by boundary stones, clearly visible to his neighbours (b), in the A.V. "landmarks". It was one of the gravest offences to "remove landmarks" (Job 24: 2), and the offender is sternly addressed in Deut. 27: 17, "Cursed be he that removeth his neighbour's landmark".

3. Hand mill. A rotating hand mill is to be found in any Palestinian farmhouse or Bedouin's tent. It consists of a fixed base stone (a) (Job 41: 15) and a top stone (b), both generally made of basalt from Bashan, and a central hole is cut through them. A small hole is bored in the top stone at a distance of about 4 or 5 cm. from the edge, into which a wooden pin (c) is inserted. The hand mill was a utensil used every day, and so the law prescribed that "no man shall take the nether or the upper millstone to pledge (Deut. 24: 6).

4. Two women of Bethlehem, grinders (Eccles. 12: 4), together turning the hand mill (Matt. 24: 41). The woman on the left is married (a); she is wearing a headdress (b) decorated with coins (c), an outer garment (d) with long sleeves (which she has turned back), and beneath it a quilted jacket (e). On the right is an unmarried woman (f), wearing a white veil (g) over her cap which has a chain of coins (h) hanging from it. Grinding is the woman's job in preparation for baking and cooking. Since morning is the time for cooking, the grinding is often done during the night, when she grinds enough flour to last one day (Prov. 31: 15). One of the women has a shallow basket (i) from which she takes corn and drops it into the hole in the upper stone. When there are two women grinding, they both have a hand on the handle, the one above the other. Since grinding was the prerogative of the woman, it is not surprising that it was a woman who threw a grindstone at Abimelech (Judges 9: 53); it was considered an insulting humiliation for a man (Judges 16: 21) or youths to be required to do the grinding (Lam. 5: 13).

14. BREAD BAKING

1. Royal bakery in ancient Egypt. In the top row a wicker sieve (*a*) and next to it a row of jars (*b*). Underneath are two slaves, each holding a stick and kneading with their feet the dough (which was otherwise kneaded by hand) in the dough-trough (*c*). Next to them are two slaves (*d*) carrying dough and a jar of oil (Lev. 2: 4) to a labourer who spreads the dough out thinly and shapes it on a table (*e*). On his right a baker's assistant (*f*) holds a ring loaf up on two rods. The pan (*g*) is covered with a flat lid with a handle; since it is hot, the cook (*h*) has a pair of tongs or something similar for lifting it off. In the top right-hand corner is a fire with a boiling-pot (*i*) where a cook is stewing fruit which he has taken from the two baskets (*j*). A servant (*k*) is bringing some more wood for the fire. Below this group is a man standing at a baker's oven (*k*). Here the baker has his hand in the oven taking the loaves out. Those that have already been removed can be seen standing on the table (*l*). There is a similar oven (*m*) in the bottom row. It is "an oven heated by the baker" (Hosea 7: 4) and it is constructed of clay in the shape of a cylinder into which wood is dropped and then lit. When it is hot, the dough in the shape of round cakes, is stuck on to the inner sides to bake. On the right the baker is bringing the dough shapes ready for baking (*n*), carrying them on a board on top of his head (cf. Genesis 40: 16). In the narrow strip above this a baker (*o*) is kneeling in front of a low table, garnishing the bread with almonds, while another baker (*p*) to his right, is dusting the bread with spices. At the bottom, on the right, is a brewery. Two men (*q, q*) are carrying a pole on their shoulders from which a jar of beer would be suspended in the part of the drawing missing in the Egyptian original. The brewers themselves (*r, r*), wearing conical caps, are working at a wicker sieve (*s*). Above them are the jars (*t, t*).

2. Baking on glowing ashes. In this method, a flat dough cake (in the shape of a pancake) was placed either on a heated stone and covered with hot ash, or between two layers of hot ash. Bread baked in this way was unleavened and had to be eaten straight away. It was this kind of "cake baken on the coals" (*a*) that was eaten by Elijah (1 Kings 19: 6) and by the Saviour with His disciples (John 21: 9, 13).

3. Baking tray. The baking tray (*a*) was a round dish of wrought iron, placed on a couple of stones over a small fire of twigs (*b*) and dung. The A.V.'s word for this tray is "pan" (Lev. 2: 5) and Moffatt, in his translation of Ezekiel 4: 3 calls it an iron plate. Standing behind the baking tray is a wooden dough dish (*c*) ("store" in the A.V.: e.g. Deut. 28: 5).

4. Baking oven. This type of baking oven (*tannoor*) was a cylinder of baked clay with a small opening at the bottom serving as an air inlet (*a*). It tapers slightly towards the top (*b*) to facilitate the application of the dough cakes to the walls by the woman baking. Next to it is an article made of wood and clay (*c*) on which to shape the dough cakes.

5. Baking oven. In this kind of oven there was a separate space for the fire (*a*) under the baking tray, which had a domed cover (*b*) over it, the front of which had an opening through which the bread was inserted (*c*). Next to the oven is a round loaf (*d*).

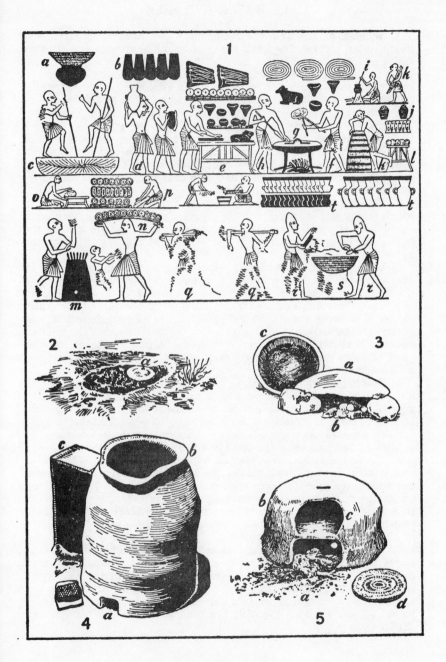

15. WATER AND MILK

1. Woman at the well. The kind of water always preferred was living water, the running fresh water of bubbling springs and streams (Song of Sol. 4: 15). It must have been a lively scene when the women came to the spring "at the time of evening, even the time that women go out to draw water" (Gen. 24: 11). When filled the pitcher was placed on the head (a). The spring (b) in the foreground is at the bottom of a deep hole dug in the ground, often right to the depth of the rock bed. The grooves in the edge have been cut by the ropes of people drawing their buckets up. The woman is wearing a white headdress (c) which can be used as a veil. For ornaments she is wearing a bracelet (d) an adornment on her forehead (e) and an ankle bracelet (g). Her long garment has been girded, i.e. it has been drawn up to about knee-level by taking a tuck at the girdle (f).

2. Bucket. The leather bucket (c) for drawing water at the well, which might rather be called a ladling bag, is fixed to a wooden cross (b) to hold it open. The well-rope or hauling line (a) is tied to the centre of the cross. Such were the buckets of old (e.g. in Numbers 24: 7; Isaiah 40: 15).

3. Water carrier. Men carried water in skins (Joshua 9: 4); a man who carried water in a pitcher was a rarity who attracted attention (Luke 22: 10). The skin bag (a) is carried on the back with the help of a rope; the stumps of the legs (b) stick out grotesquely. The water carrier is wearing a cloth wound round his head (c), trousers (d), an outer garment not unlike a nightshirt (e) and sandals (f). Sandals fastened with latchets (or straps) (Gen. 14: 23) were the commonest form of footwear in ancient times (1 Kings 2: 5; Ezek. 24: 17, 23; 2 Chron. 28: 15).

4. Butter making. F. J. Bruijel in *Bijbel en Natuur* writes: Fresh milk as we know it is used very little since for the greater part of the year it is impossible to keep it for any time without its turning sour. It is used almost exclusively for children. The Old Testament word "milk" generally corresponds to the Hebrew *chālāb*, a kind of milk which has had rennet added to it to curdle it and has been left to go sour by fermentation, resulting in something comparable to junket and yoghurt. It was from this *chālāb* that *chem'a*, butter, was made. For this, three poles (a) were pushed into the ground to form a tripod on which a goatskin bag (b) containing the *chālāb* was hung. The woman then sat down near the bag and subjected it to a battery of well-aimed punches. (It would be more accurate to interpret the word "churning" in Proverbs 30: 33 by punching or thumping). As a result the contents were continually being shaken up and the thumping brought about the conversion of the milk into butter. Apart from thick, sour milk, fresh curdled milk was also known. By separating the water from it, cheese was produced, cf. Job 10: 10, ". . . and curdled me like cheese". The woman is wearing full-length garments, a skirt (c), a jacket (d) and an open coat (e); her head is covered with a veil tied with a band (f).

16. HUNTING AND FISHING

1. Hunting nets. (Relief on a monument at Hermel, in Syria). An animal (*a*) that got caught up in a barrier (*b*) could be taken captive in a hunting net (*c*), which could be thrown over the animal's head on the end of two sticks (*d*). In Isaiah 51: 20 an animal is referred to (the Hebrew word can mean antelope, or, in earlier translations, onyx or wild bull), as being caught in such a net; the prophet compares the men who have fainted and are lying at the head of all the streets, to a wild bull in a net. The prophet Ezekiel reminds us that the net was cast widespread by the hunter in God's warning to Juda and its king: "My net also will I spread upon him" (Ezek. 12: 13).

2. Bird snaring. (Egyptian drawing). Two Egyptians are drawing in the clap-net (*a*) in which they have caught birds large and small as Hosea 7: 12 tells us: I will spread my net upon them; I will bring them down as the fowls of the heaven.

3. Angling (Egyptian drawing). An angler in a loin-cloth (*a*) is holding a fishing-rod (*b*) with a line (*c*), hook and bait (cf. Isaiah 19: 8). Angling was not restricted to the Nile, for there were fishing-grounds specially maintained by means of sluices ("sluices and ponds for fish", Isa. 19: 10). The angler sitting on his haunches has a line but no rod. This method of fishing was and still is customary on Lake Gennesareth: "cast the hook" (Matt. 17: 27).

4. Fishermen (Egyptian drawing). The calmly flowing waters of Egypt abounded in fish. A profitable fishing industry was the result. The Israelites cherished memories of it when they were in the desert ("we remember the fish which we did eat in Egypt freely", Num. 11: 5). The fish were caught with a hook, pierced with a spear or caught in a drag-net. The net (*b*), weighted with stones (*c*), and held by long ropes (*a*), was lowered for a while and then drawn in again.

5. Fishing in the Sea of Galilee. In the background the rocky slopes rise steeply from the water's edge; this is the mountainous country of Golan or Gaulanitis (*a*). The fisherman standing out in the water is tending the drag-net, the cork floats (*b*) of which can be seen floating on the surface. The men in the foreground are drawing the net (*c*) in. It is this sort of net which catches all the fish within its wide sweep and not just one or two individually as in line fishing, to which the kingdom of heaven is likened in Matthew 13: 47. Fishermen were lightly clad in ancient times, in fact, they stripped (John 21: 7), wearing only a short shirt. We read of St. Peter that he girt his fisher's coat unto him and leaped into the sea. Some people have thought it strange that Peter should have returned to the shore in his wet clothes, but we must bear in mind that it can be very hot in these parts. Sven Hedin recorded a temperature of 87° here on July 26th, and the Swedish traveller used to enjoy the delicious feeling of his thin clothing drying in the wind after he had poured handfuls of water over himself.

6. Fishing with cast-net (*a*): a round net approximately four metres wide, which is cast over the water with a wide sweep (Ezek. 26: 5; Matt. 4: 18; John 21: 6).

17. CRAFTS

1. Leather dressing (Egyptian drawing). At the top, left, is a worker (*a*) using a sharp stone to scrape the bristles off a hide, which he is holding steady with his feet. Underneath, a worker is cutting leather into straps (*b*), while a third is holding the leather tight (*c*). Next to them a hide is being stretched taut over a frame (*d*); above it, a dressed hide (*e*). To the right of this is a man passing on finished articles (*f*). Various things were made of leather, such as sandals (*g*), parts of harness (*h*) and covers for official documents (*i*).

2. Potter working at the wheel (Egyptian drawing). First potter (*a*) has a lump of clay (*c*) on the wheel (*b*). He is shaping the inside of the vessel with his hands. Some vessels (*d, e, f, g, h, i*) are finished. The second potter (*j*) is shaping the outside of a pitcher, his left hand holding the base (*k*). A third potter (*l*) has just finished his vessel (*m*). The last potter has started to work on a lump of clay (*n*): "as the clay is in the potter's hands" (Jer. 18:6) "he wrought a work on the wheels", (Jer. 18:3).

3. Potters at the oven (Egyptian illustration). The first figure (*a*) is shaping a flat plate of clay in his hands; another (*b*) is stoking the fire in the oven (*c*); a third man (*d*) is handing the shapes to the potter (*e*) dressed in a girdle (*f*) only; he places these shapes on the hot oven. The finished pieces of pottery are taken away by a labourer with a yoke (*g*).

4. Barber at work. 5. Barber's razor. In ancient times the barber practised his trade in the open air, in the shade of a tree. He bound the hair up at the top of the scalp and cut the hair short near the temples or shaved it off. The customer meanwhile sat on a three-legged stool (*a*) with a soap-dish (*b*) in front of him. For shaving and hair-cutting the barber used a "barber's razor" (fig. 5) "to pass upon the head and upon the beard" (Ezek. 5:1)—despite its very strange shape.

18. VINEYARDS AND OLIVE PRESS

1. Watchman's booth in the vineyard. In the fruit gardens (for instance, in the garden of cucumbers, Isa. 1: 8), and in the vineyards there were small shelters not unlike summer-houses, for use during the ripening of the fruit and the harvest. These consisted of a roof made of branches supported on rough posts. They are watchmen's booths (b) on top of the watch towers (a) built in the vineyard (Isa. 5: 2), and at harvest-time the whole family would often live in such a booth (the cottage in the vineyard, Isa. 1: 8). The booth also occurs in the Bible as a symbol of protection (Ps. 27: 5). These structures naturally fall into a state of dilapidation and collapse in time, and it is to this that the promise refers in Amos 9: 11.

2. Grape harvest : grape treading (Egyptian drawing). On the right is a bower of vines (a), beneath which pickers (b) are cutting off the bunches of grapes (c). On the left is the bath of the wine-press (d) in which the men are standing, treading the grapes (e). To one side, the wine flows from the bath into a stone tank (f). Later, the wine will be bottled in jars (g).

3. Treading in the wine-press. "The treading of wine-presses" was well-known of old (Neh. 13: 15) and there is the famous reference in Isaiah's vision: "Wherefore art thou red in thine apparel, and thy garments like him that treadeth in the winefat? I have trodden the winepress alone" (Isa. 63: 2, 3). In addition to the bath of the wine-press (a), there was also the trough, which Moffatt calls the vintage (in Jer. 48: 33). There were two ways of pressing the grapes, either by means of levering a heavy weight onto them, or by treading them with the bare feet in the bath of the wine-press (a), whence the trodden wine flowed into a lower trough or gutter (b) running to the bath of the press.

4. 5. Olive press. Olive oil was used in God's service: (1) as "oil for the light"; (2) as "oil for the holy anointing"; (3) as part of the meat offering. The oil used for the lamps and for holy unction is described as "pure olive oil beaten" and that used for the meat offering as "beaten oil" (Exod. 27: 20; 29: 40; Lev. 24: 2; Num. 28: 5). This oil was extracted from olives specially selected for their excellent quality, by crushing them into a pulpy substance in a stone mortar and then hanging the pulp in baskets so that the oil was strained through. This oil which drips from the basket and is now quite clear and free of particles of pulp or pips is what is referred to as "pure beaten oil". It is colourless and burns without giving off smoke. If now the process is continued by placing some weight on the pulp in the basket, in the form of stones or a wooden block, further oil is obtained of a slightly inferior, but still very good quality, "the beaten oil". In order to extract oil for everyday use, the pulp was compressed still further, and in this process the pips were crushed as well. Oil obtained in this way was far less pure, containing as it did particles of fruit and pips. The olive press (a) used for this purpose consisted of a heavy, round stone base, with a circular gutter hollowed out of its face, in which a heavy stone wheel (b) turned as it was swung round at the end of an arm on a pivot (c). No mention is made of this olive press in the Bible, except in the one reference in Job 24: 11, "which make oil within their walls".

19. SHEPHERDS, SHEEP, STABLES

1. Shepherd with club and staff. The club (*a*) was usually made of oak, about 2 feet long, and with a knob at the end about the size of an orange. A loop through the handle enabled it to be hung from the girdle or slung from the wrist like a whip. The staff (*b*) was four to six feet long and was generally made from a peeled vine branch. The staff proved useful to the shepherd when climbing, for slashing twigs or leaves, for strafing lingering or fighting goats and to lean on when keeping watch over his flocks. This shepherd is wearing a long garment (*c*), fastened with a girdle (*g*), underneath a kind of cloak (*d*). His head-cloth (*e*) is fixed with an akal (*f*), and he is holding a sling in his right hand.

2. Sling. This was normally of twined wool, with a wider centre-piece, about two inches wide, specially reinforced to take the stone which is flung out "as out of the middle of a sling" (1 Sam. 25: 29). The stones used were the small "smooth stones" (1 Sam. 17: 40) found in the summer on the dry river beds by the shepherds who collected them in their "shepherd's bags".

3. Shepherd's boy with sling. After placing the stone in the sling, the middle finger of the right hand was put through the eye of the loop, while the other, somewhat thinner end, was held in the same hand which now whirled the sling above the head. The art lay in letting go of the line at precisely the right moment so that the stone would hit the target.

4. Shepherd's boy playing the flute. A favourite pastime among the shepherd boys was playing the shawm (*a*) to their flocks. They made these out of reeds. They had six holes, and the boy used three fingers of each hand to play. There may be a reference to this in the Bible, where Moffatt describes shepherds as having an "ear for pastoral notes" (Judges 5: 16).

5. Sheep-folds. The sheep-folds served to provide shelter for the sheep on summer nights. These were in fact simply enclosures with walls of loosely stacked stones, which also provided protection against "thieves and robbers" (John 10: 1). In the wall was an opening, "the door in the sheepfold" (*a*), and it was here that the "porter" lay, usually one of the shepherds. In the morning he opened the door, and the shepherds called their sheep.

6. Solomon's stables at Megiddo. It was said of Solomon that he had "cities of store, and cities for his chariots and cities for his horsemen" (1 Kings 9: 19) and he used to take his horses to the north to sell them to the Hittite and Syrian kings (1 Kings 10: 29). They were moved *via* the trade route on which Megiddo lay. And so it was that Solomon's stables were found in the course of the excavations here. The stables were built ranged along both sides of a long central passage. The roof was supported on two rows of stone pillars, between which stone mangers were placed. The pillars had holes in them so that ropes could be pulled through them when the animals were tied up.

20. SMITH; WEAVER

1. Smith. Egyptian drawing of a smith with a blowpipe to blow the fire (*a*) and a pair of tongs (*b*) with which to remove the iron articles from the fire. It is the smith who blows the coals in the fire (Isa. 54: 16). The blacksmith in making an axe works in the coals and fashions it with hammers (Isa. 44: 12, using marginal note).

2 and 3. Horizontal loom. 4. Vertical loom. The horizontal loom was assembled in between the cloth beam (*b*) and the yarn beam (*a*). The shuttle, which weaves the weft into the warp runs between the warp threads. This is what Job 7: 6 refers to: "my days are swifter than a weaver's shuttle and are spent without hope". At the time of the Old Testament, weaving was a woman's job; her hands hold the weaver's spindle (Prov. 31: 19). Delilah was using a horizontal loom when she wove Samson's hair at a weaver's beam (Judges 16: 13, 14). In 1 Samuel 17: 7, however, reference is made to a standing loom: "And the shaft of his spear was like a weaver's beam". The act of cutting off the yarn when the cloth is finished is used by the prophet as a metaphor for the ending of man's life: "he will cut me off from the thrum" (Isa. 38: 12, margin). Thrum here means the remainder of the weaver's yarn which is cut off, so that Hezekiah said in effect, God has cut me off, just as a weaver cut off the finished cloth from the attached thread-ends. This confirms what has been said earlier: "I have cut off like a weaver my life" (i.e. by my sins).

5. Syrian weaver at his loom, carrying on the trade associated with St. Paul, who was a tent maker (Acts 18: 3). It is sometimes thought that the making of tents consisted of the weaving of tent cloth from the famous Cilician goat hair. Another view holds that Paul cut the woven material into strips and sewed these into tents, while there are also those who maintain that tent-making was associated with the leather trade.

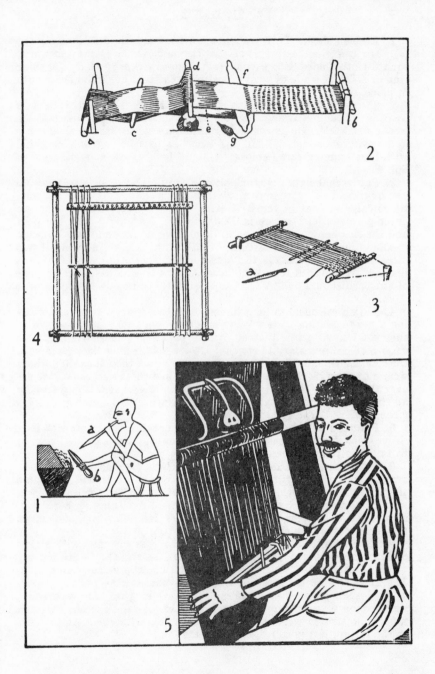

47

21. DRESS

1. Arabian sheik. This Arab wears a wide mantle with long sleeves (*a*). He has the headwear of the Bedouins, a large greyish-white, square cloth folded into a triangle, the so-called *keffiyeh* (*b*). A thick ring or *fakal* (*c*) made of wool or twisted goat hair holds the head-cloth in place.

2. Shepherd from the region round Bethlehem. The shepherd is wearing an undergarment (*a*) bound with a girdle (*c*), over which has a cloak (*b*). He is walking on rough, sharp stones shod only in a pair of sandals (*f*). In his arms he is carrying a young kid with long hanging ears (Amos 3: 12) and long, black hair (cf. Song of Sol. 6: 5).

3. Patriarchal figure with cloak and staff. The man is wearing an undergarment (*a*) gathered up with a girdle (*b*). This robe is sometimes called a coat in the A.V. (Gen. 37: 3). Over this he wears an outer garment (*c*) (vesture in Deut. 22: 12). At night-time the poor and the shepherds used it to wrap themselves up in, and for this reason it should not be pledged after nightfall (Deut. 24: 13). At work it was often taken off (Matt. 24: 18; Acts 7: 58). The head-cloth (*d*) here is just a scarf wrapped round the head. On his feet he has a simple type of strapped sandal (*e*). A full-length staff (*f*) completes his equipment (Gen. 38: 18).

4. Jewish prisoners in long tunics. The two women (*a, a*) are wearing a head-covering with a long veil at the back (*b*) reaching down to their ankles. As a rule the veil did not cover their faces (Gen. 12: 14; 24: 15, 16); if necessary they could always hold it over their faces with their hands (Gen. 24: 65). This veil was worn over their tunics (*c*), which were also worn by the men (*d*). The tunics had short sleeves (*e*). Whenever they wished to move quickly, they would gather this garment up at the front; "gird up your loins" (2 Kings 4: 29), or "your loins girded" (Exod. 12: 11).

5. Farmer's wife from Samaria, in a long white garment with long sleeves (*khurkah*) (*a*), a white veil (*b*) and on top of it a padded ring (*c*) to take the pitcher when it was carried on the head.

6. Egyptian in a loin-cloth. The loin-cloth (*a*) was very common among both the Egyptians and the Babylonians. It had the same shape as the sack-cloth, a coarse piece of goat-hair or camel-hair cloth, which was worn next to the skin as a sign of mourning (Job 16: 15), sometimes as the sole article of clothing (1 Kings 20: 31), sometimes under the outer garment (2 Kings 6: 30).

7. 8. Sandals. Footwear consisted of sandals fastened with straps or latchets (Gen. 14: 23; Isa. 5: 27; Mark 1: 7). They were usually made of leather, but were very simple and of little value (Amos 2: 6). The sandals were taken off on entering a house or holy place (Exod. 3: 5; Joshua 5: 15). At all other times, walking on bare feet was a sign of mourning (2 Sam. 15: 30; Ezek. 24: 17, 23). The old Assyrian sandals illustrated were actually heel-caps (*a*), with their straps fixed to the instep, the so-called shoe latchets (*b*).

49

22. ORNAMENTS

1. Necklace from Ras Shamrah. Among the discoveries at the excavations in Ugarit (Ras Shamrah) was this necklace which, from its position, could be given a date in the fourteenth century B.C. It is made up of beads of gold, silver, cornelian, amber and pearls, and it has in addition a number of pendants (*a*). Such necklaces were very popular at the time; they were worn in ancient Israel ("tablets" in Exodus 35: 22; "chains about thy neck" in Proverbs 1: 9; "ornaments of fine gold" in Proverbs 25: 12; "chains of gold" in Song of Sol. 1: 10). Half moons and small bottles of perfume served as pendants (Isa. 3: 18, 19).

2. A mirror (Egyptian silver mirror from Byblos in Syria). The hand mirrors consisted of cast, convex metal, often silver (and so Elihu speaks of the sky which is strong as a molten looking-glass, Job 37: 18). Sometimes it was made of other metals ("and he made the laver of brass and the foot of it of brass, of the looking glasses of the women assembling", Exod. 38: 8).

3. Egyptian woman, using make-up, a mirror (*a*) in her left hand. "She painted her face and tired her head" (2 Kings 9: 30). Their preference was for *galena* or *stibium*. This was applied with a brush to their eyebrows and lashes to make the eye-balls seem whiter and the eyes larger ("though thou rentest thy eyes with painting", Jer. 4: 30; "paintedst thy eyes", Ezek. 23: 40).

4. An instrument for crushing make-up powder (Teleilât el-Ghassul). *Stibium* was rubbed out with oil or ointment to be used as powder. It was then kept in make-up jars such as were found at the excavations at Shechem; the name of Job's youngest daughter, Keren happûch, can have the meaning make-up horn or casket (Job 42: 14).

5. Ear-ring from Megiddo. Ear-rings (Gen. 35: 4; Num. 31: 50) were worn by women and children ("the golden ear-rings which are in the ears of your wives, of your sons and of your daughters", Exod. 32: 2).

6. Signet ring found in Jericho. As early as the time of the patriarchs the signet ring was known (Gen. 38: 18); the signet ring was used instead of a signature. Sometimes it was worn by the Israelites on a cord round their necks (Gen. 38: 18, Moffatt, "'your signet-ring,' she said, 'your cord for it . . .'"), by the Egyptians it was worn on the finger (Gen. 41: 42) as it was, later on, by the Israelites too ("the signet upon my right hand", Jer. 22: 24).

7. Signet of "Shema, servant of Jeroboam" at Megiddo. A roaring lion is depicted in the middle of the seal, and the inscription reads: Shema servant of Jeroboam. This Jeroboam might be the second king of that name who ruled in Samaria between 783 and 743 B.C. and who had an official by the name of Shema. The signet is made of jaspar and it clearly demonstrates the high standard of engraving at that time.

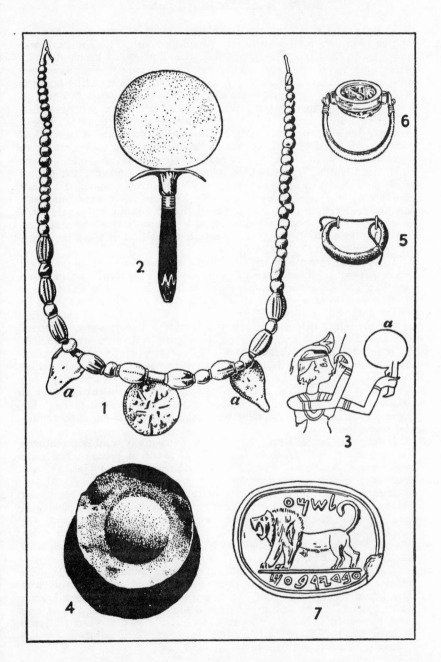

23. MUSICAL INSTRUMENTS

1. Harp at Ur. This harp is an instrument of eleven strings (*a*), strung obliquely across an ornate sounding-board (*b*). The harp was played with the hand (1 Sam. 16: 16, "he shall play with his hand"). In Israel a harpist would play walking, so that the harp could not have been of a very great size (1 Sam. 10: 5; 2 Sam. 6: 5). The sounding-board is decorated with mosaic and there is a ram's-head ornament at one end.

2. Jewish prisoners playing the lyre. The prisoners, probably men of Judah from Lachish, are on their way through a mountain forest, guarded by a soldier carrying a club (*b*) in his hand and a bag full of bows on his back (*d*). The prisoners are wearing long tunics and have bare feet. One of them is bare-headed, the others are wearing caps with head-bands. They have obviously Jewish features; the cut of their hair and their short, thick beards. They were compelled to play the lyre (*c*) on their journey (Ps. 137: 3, "for they that carried us away captive required of us a song"). The soldier is wearing boots (*a*); these Assyrian soldiers' boots are mentioned in Isaiah 9: 5: "the stamping warrior's boot, the bloodstained war-attire, shall all of them be burnt, as fuel for the fire" (Moffatt).

3. Assyrian cymbal-player. A cymbal consisted of two brass bowls (*a*) (Ps. 150: 5, "loud cymbals"), which could be struck against one another, not for accompaniment but to beat the rhythm. They were used in *ensembles* (1 Chron. 25: 1; 2 Chron. 5: 12; Ezra 3: 10), and in processions (2 Sam. 6: 5).

4. Assyrian kettle-drums. In the temple kettle-drums or timpani the height of a man were played, and their dull tones were audible at a great distance. There were also portable kinds, cylindrical or conical which, like the larger versions, were beaten with the knuckles or fingers. In Israel the hand-drum or tambourine was often played by women (Exod. 15: 20); it was the favourite instrument at national feasts, for processions or on joyful occasions, and served to beat the time for the singing, especially when this was combined with round-dancing (Judges 11: 34).

5. Assyrian double flute. The flute was originally, and is sometimes still made of reed. In later times it was made of bronze. The flute was used a great deal, primarily to accompany dirges (Jer. 48: 36; Matt. 9: 23) and songs of joy.

6. Egyptian girl playing the lute. The girl has a ribbon (*a*) round her head and a flower in her hair. She is playing a lute (*b*) with a plectrum. The strings of the lute are plucked with this, a small chip, which was often used to play early string instruments. The lute had a pear-shaped back, and those belonging to wealthy Israelites were made of sandalwood (1 Kings 10: 12).

7. Roundel with musical instruments (Egyptian painting). The women with palm branches (*a*), tambourines (*b*) and lyres (*c*) accompany the dance with music, while a naked child stands near with a branch in its hand. Dances with music at religious feasts were, of course, also well known in Israel ("if the daughters of Shiloh come out to dance in dances", Judges 21: 21); in the centre of the illustration are the "damsels playing with timbrels" (Ps. 68: 25).

52

53

24. SCRIPT (1)

1, 2. Clay tablet found at the excavations at Shechem. Two tablets with cuneiform characters were found at Shechem. "Although small and unpretentious and difficult to decypher, these types of inscriptions are of the utmost importance for our knowledge of the life and thought of the ancient Canaanites during the centuries before the arrival of the Israelites. Both tablets have writing on both sides. The second (depicted here) is a business letter, slightly importunate in tone. The writer asks for a consignment of corn and best quality oil, the same that he had received three years previously, and wants to know whether it is his fault that he has heard nothing, since his agents have also written repeatedly" (Prof. Dr. Th. Böhl).

3. Israel-stele found in the ruins of Pharaoh Merenptah's Temple of the Dead near Thebes. This inscription, in hieroglyphics, is called an Israel-stele because it mentions the name Israel. The top part is divided into two halves: in the centre is the god Amon under the winged orb of the sun, handing a sickle-like sword to the king with his right hand and holding a sceptre in his left. The king is wearing a battle helmet. Standing behind the king on the right is the falcon-headed god Horus, on the left the goddess Mut. Below this is Merenptah's inscription. It is a song "to make known to all lands everywhere (Merenptah's conquests in every land) and to show forth the fairness of his deeds". It is dated the third day of the eleventh month of the fifth year of Merenptah's reign, which is around the year 1228 B.C. In the song the king boasts that

Israel's people are few; his seed exists no more.

(It is a photographic reproduction; part of the illustration appears in a larger scale on the front cover.)

4. Axe at Ras Shamrah inscribed in alphabetic cuneiform characters. In the course of the excavations at Ras Shamrah in Phoenicia, many interesting finds have thrown a new light on the life of the Phoenicians at the time of Moses, one such discovery being that alphabetic script is older than had been hitherto supposed. At Ras Shamrah an alphabet was found consisting of 29 letters. The decyphering was accomplished surprisingly quickly, and the script transpired to be simple compared with the cuneiform characters.

5. Samaritan scroll. At each end is a wooden roller called the "tree of life" with ornate ends, decorated at the top with ornamental finials or crowns (*a*). The roll is wound round these two pins in such a way that whatever had so far that year already been read was wound on one pin, while the other pin held the part that was still to be read. A precious cover (*b*) of silk or other valuable material was wrapped round the scroll of the law.

The Pentateuch of the Samaritans is written in Hebrew, which was to them the sacred language, the language of the law. The alphabetic script, however, is not the well-known square script, but has more in common with the old Phoenician characters.

There is evidence in the Bible of the scroll form of these ancient books (Ezra 6: 2; Isa. 8: 1; Jer. 36: 2; Ezek. 2: 9; Zach. 5: 1).

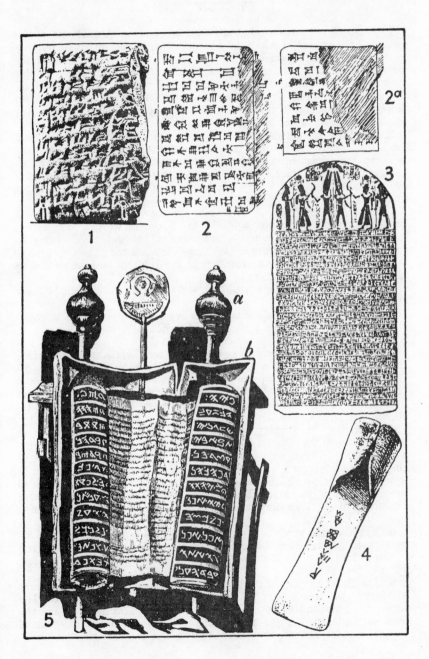

1

2

2ᵃ

3

a

b

5

4

25. SCRIPT (2)

1. Potsherd with an inscription found in Samaria. Under one of the rooms of the palace of Ahab, in a rock cellar, 75 fragments of pottery with inscriptions in ancient Hebrew script were unearthed. They were written in black ink with a stylus, and proved to be similar to way-bills, which accompanied the consignments of wine and oil for the royal stores. It says in this letter "in the year fifteen from Abiezer to Asa (the son of) Ahimelech (a consignment of wine for) Baalah (resident in) El Mattan".

2. Ostrakon or potsherd at Tell-ed-Duweir (probably the biblical Lachish). The writing is in ink which, according to chemical analysis, is composed of an extract of gall-nuts and soot. It is a "letter" to the commander of the fortress of Lachish of the year 588 B.C. (shortly before Nebuchadnezzar's siege and victory, *viz.* Jer. 34: 7). The letter is servile in its tone.

"To my master Ya'ush.—That Jehovah may grant my master good news at this moment, even now. What is your servant, who is a dog, that my master should think of his servant? May Jehovah bring to perdition those who venture upon things of which they have no understanding." (There is also an instance in the Bible of an inferior calling himself a dog, 1 Sam. 24: 14.)

3. Seal belonging to Gedaliah. This seal too bears the ancient Hebrew script; it reads

> (seal) of Gedaliah
> who (rules) over the house.

This is then the property of one of the three Gedaliahs, whose name means Jehovah-is-great, who were respectively "the singer of David" (1 Chron. 25: 3), a contemporary of Jeremiah's (Jer. 38: 1), or Ahikam's son (2 Kings 25: 22). This last is considered the most probable. Here he bears the title: the one in charge of the house, the lord of the palace, the deputy ruler of the land.

4. Container for keeping letters. In the days of Jeremiah letters were written on "a roll of a book" (Jer. 36: 2) which could be cut with a pen-knife (Jer. 36: 23). Apart from these, there was the tablet of clay to which letters were applied with a "pen" (Isa. 8: 1), "a pen of iron" (Jer. 17: 1). This is also how we must imagine the "deeds of purchase" (Jer. 32: 11). These letters were kept in an earthenware container, of which an illustration is given, reproduced from a specimen found at Taanach.

5. Egyptian scribe writing out "a deed", holding a "stylus" in his hand, with two more behind his ears. Professional scribes were employed by kings and merchants in early times (2 Sam. 8: 17; Ps. 45: 1; Isa. 33: 18; Jer. 36: 26).

6. Jewish transcriber of the Torah. A Torah roll (with the five books of Moses) was transcribed on parchment with the utmost care. The scribe not only had to be able to write well, he also had to have the spiritual understanding to enable him to carry out the sacred task of copying the Torah.

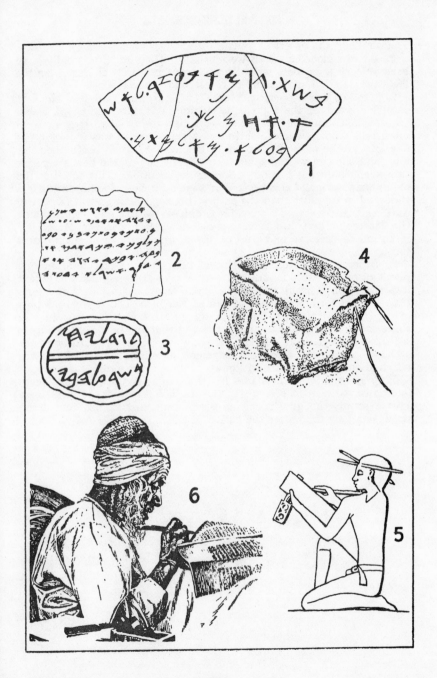

1

2

3

4

6

5

The scrolls in the desert of Juda.

1. Jar in which the scrolls were packed. There must originally have been at least 51 of these jars with their contents; they all date from the Hellenistic period and belong to the second century B.C.

2. Scroll of Isaiah open at column 32 (right) and 33 (left). The first complete word of the right-hand column is the beginning of Isaiah 39: 9. The column on the left shows Isaiah 40: 2b–28a. It is a parchment roll. The cave in which the scrolls were found was some kind of depository; the collection probably belonged to some brotherhood or sect, and one can well imagine the owners bringing the books here for safe keeping during a time of war or persecution. This scroll is the oldest manuscript of this book that has so far been found, and it is a thousand years older than the earliest text of Isaiah known (at Cairo) until this discovery. It provides proof of the accuracy with which the Masoretic text has been handed down. It was the Masoretes' intention to preserve and pass on the sacred writings in their purest form.

3, 4. Scraps with fragments of texts in Phoenician characters. Among pieces of manuscripts found in the cave were also fragments of a text in archaic (Old Phoenician) script, which shows a great deal of resemblance in its form with the ostraka at Lachish. The text forms part of the "Law of Holiness" (a name given to Lev. 17: 1–26: 46. In this section of the Old Testament the fact that the Lord God is holy is repeatedly emphasized, e.g. in Lev. 19: 2; 20: 7, 26). According to the archaeologist R. de Vaux, these fragments date from the fourth century B.C. and they are the earliest known biblical manuscripts.

5. Fragments with the name El (the name for God) in the fourth line down, written in Phoenician script. The remainder is in Hebrew square script, though Phoenician script remained in use for sacred writings a long time after the period of exile.

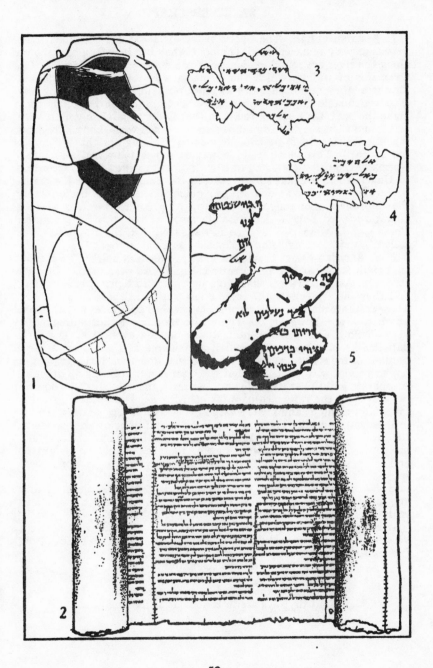

27. RIVER CRAFT

1. Assyrian guffah. The Greek historian Herodotus described these vessels as very remarkable. "The boats they use for going to Babylon along the river are round in shape and are made entirely of leather (*a*). Over ribs of willow, which the Armenians had been ordered to cut for them, they stretched hides as an outer skin, without making any clearly definable stern or tapering at all towards the bow, but they make the boat like a shield, round in shape, they completely fill it with reeds, and then they let it go down-stream laden with goods. The boat is steered with oars (*b*) by two oarsmen (*c*) standing upright." (Herodotus I: 194.) This illustration, however, shows four men all seated. Normally the cargo consisted of barrels of palm wine. Here (according to Unger) there are screws (*d*) or screw-like implements for the transportation of human-headed winged bulls of limestone. Undoubtedly the impressive monuments yielded by Assyrian excavations are the gigantic winged bulls which were stationed at the royal palace gates. These *guffahs* were also used as ferries (a city on the Euphrates was called "ferry" or "crossing", Tiphsah, I Kings 4: 24).

2, 3. Assyrian kelek; 2. ancient kelek; 3. modern kelek. "We know that right from earliest times rafts called keleks were used. They are shown on Assyrian reliefs that have just come to light at excavations, and they show precisely the same construction as those in use today. These rafts are made of poplar trunks (*a*) stacked criss-cross on top of one another. Since, however, the Tigris with its many rapids is frequently very shallow, an ingenious method was devised even at a very early date for keeping the rafts as high as possible in the water: a large number of inflated rams' skins (*b*) were tied underneath the grating of poplar trunks, with the result that the craft had practically no draught. A separate guild plies its trade on these rafts, the kelekdjis (*c*) who propel and steer the raft with oars (*d*). On the kelek is an 'ark', a cabin for shelter at night and for the cargo" (I. Guyer, *Meine Tigrisfahrt*).

4. Egyptian craft. The drawing is an illustration of an episode in the story of Cheops. This king desired a skilful magician to attend his court. Then barques were rigged, that the king's son might go and fetch the magician. At the meeting many courteous words were spoken. The magician was willing to accompany the king's son and said: "Let a boat be given to me, that I may take with me my pupils and books." Then he was given two boats with their crews. This is the scene depicted in the illustration.

In early times the Nile teemed with barques and all kinds of different vessels. "The daytime and the waters", one of the songs of Ichnaton, exclaims:

> The barques sail upstream and downstream,
> Every route is open, because thou art risen,
> The fish in the river leap up before thee,
> And thy rays are in the midst of the great sea.

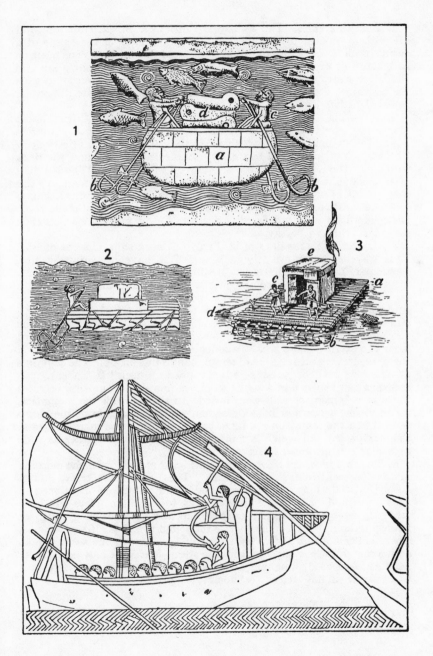

28. SHIPS

1. Philistine ships. The Philistine ships were finished off fore and aft with a vertical prow and sternpost (*a*), carved in the shape of a swan's neck (*b*). They were sailing ships, and had no oars. The mast (*c*) had a top or crow's-nest (*d*). On the lower of the two ships are two Philistine warriors (*e*), both carrying the round shield associated with their armies. One of them is also carrying a characteristic dagger (*g*) in his right hand.

2. Phoenician ship. The ships had a curved shape with almost identically similar stems and sternposts. The masts (*a*) had yardarms (*b*), and the abundance of ropes used in the yard rigging is also typical. The ships had high wash-boards (*c*), strakes built up round the deck to prevent the deck cargo from slipping off in high seas. The building of such ships is described in Ezekiel 27: 5ff, "they have made all thy ship boards of fir trees of Senir: they have taken cedars from Lebanon to make masts for thee. Of the oaks of Bashan have they made thine oars; fine linen with broidered work from Egypt was that which thou spreadest forth to be thy sail".

3. Grain ship in the days of St. Paul. "A corn ship, like the one St. Paul travelled in, can safely be assumed to have been quite a size. Particulars have been preserved of ships with a tonnage of 2,600 tons. St. Paul's ship could accommodate 276 men. The hull ran up to a bird's-head carving above the bows and the tail of a bird at the stern. Amidships was a high mast, usually of cedar wood (cf. also Ezek. 27: 5), and near the prow a smaller one for hoisting a small sail. Steering was accomplished by means of two large oars, trailing to port and starboard from the stern. There was a wooden hut for the helmsman built on the deck, serving also as a small temple containing an idol. The captain's quarters lay aft; the passengers bivouacked on deck" (I. Snoek).

4. Seamen at work in a rising wind. A mural at Pompeii illustrates the way in which the sails were furled. In the centre is the mainmast, made in one piece and held by strong ropes running from the ship's sides up to the main top. A large yard is fixed to the mainmast, and this carries the sail which is reinforced with strips of leather as wide as a man's hand and sewn across it.

5. The ship in which St. Paul travelled lying at anchor on the morning of the fourteenth day of the storm. "The English authority, Smith, has calculated that a ship sailing under the conditions mentioned in Acts 27 would need just fourteen days to get from Crete to Malta (cf. Acts 27: 33ff). When they cast the lead it revealed a depth of twenty fathoms. After a short while the sounding is less, fifteen fathoms. There is some alarm that they may run aground, so the seamen take action and drop four anchors from the stern; four since only small sheet anchors were used, weighing about 55 lb. each. Then the passengers had to wait till daybreak" (I. Snoek).

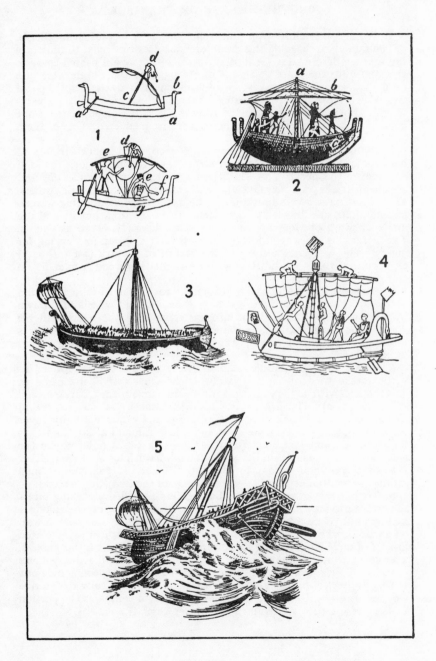

29. OTHER MEANS OF TRANSPORT

1. Women travelling. Assyrian relief in the palace of Sennacherib. The famous archaeologist Alfred Jeremias uses this relief to illustrate the journey described in Genesis 12: 6: "And Abraham passed through the land unto the place of Shechem." Originally the wheels were just solid discs of wood. Spokes are of a much later date. This type of two-wheeled cart also dates from that period; it was built by cartwrights, most of whom were Elamites. The two women in the front both wear caps with veils, but their faces are uncovered. One of them is holding a pitcher.

2. Philistine ox-carts. Philistines can be recognized from their plumed helmets (*a*), tied on with cords or straps, and having a cloth that fell down over the neck. The Philistines are armed with lances (*b*) and daggers (*c*). They are portrayed here waging war against the Egyptians. The Philistine shield is round (*d*). The ox-carts (*e*), containing women and children, are drawn by four oxen. They are square-built and are made of wood or woven wattles. Wooden discs (*f*) served as wheels. The women in the wagon are holding up their children and crying for mercy. The well-known story of the return of the ark (1 Sam. 6: 7) also confirms that the Philistine wagon was made of wood (1 Sam. 6: 14) and drawn by oxen.

3. Carts used by the Takkarri (an Asiatic race referred to in Egyptian writings). They are riding in carts with heavy solid wheels (*a*), drawn by four oxen (*b*). One of the drovers is goading the oxen with his stick; the other man, looking round, has a round shield (*c*). The carts are square with wooden sides. The woman in the cart is holding a child under its arms.

4. Camel saddles. Saddled camels (Gen. 37: 25) are mentioned as early as the time of the patriarchs. The Queen of Sheba came to Jerusalem "with a very great train, with camels that bare spices" (1 Kings 10: 2). The Bible refers to swift camels (Isa. 66: 20; 60: 6) as well as to these pack-camels. A riding camel would normally cover three to four miles in an hour for eight to ten hours a day, and that for weeks on end. No horse could achieve that. In order to tie the load on well, unusual saddles were fitted. Two long sticks on either side of the animal served to increase the carrying surface. Camel saddles were often kept in the women's part of the tent (Gen. 31: 34).

5. Track between stone walls. The traders travelled along big international caravan routes (Gen. 37: 25), and the lonely traveller along a hollow path (Num. 22: 24) running through the vineyards with a wall on each side of it. Gardens, orchards, vineyards and sometimes isolated groups of olive trees and fig trees were enclosed by walls (*a*) or *gedhers*. The *gedhers* were built of rough pieces of rock, and the dusty holes in these loosely constructed walls often offered a welcome hide-out to snakes (Eccles. 10: 8). The *gedher* was used metaphorically to describe God's protection (Ezra 9: 9; Micah 7: 11). David compares the portion of the godless to a wall ruined by winter gales (Ps. 62: 3).

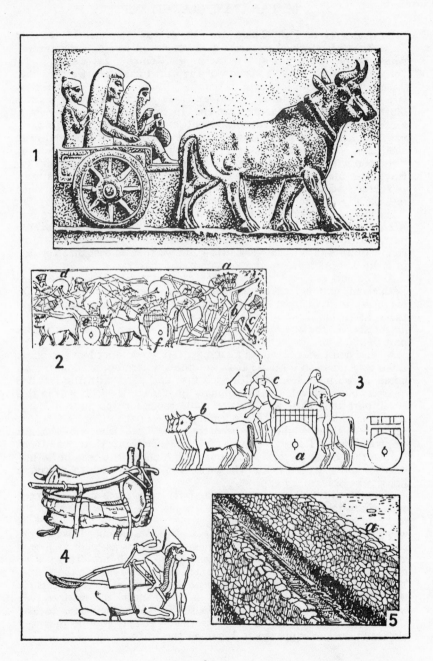

30. CARAVANSERAI OR INN

Caravanserai or inn. There are one or two passages in the Old Testament in which there are references to an inn or caravanserai, where people could put up for the night (Gen. 43: 21; Exod. 4: 24; Jer. 9: 2). In St. Luke's version of the Christmas story we read that "there was no room for them in the inn" (Luke 2: 7). A caravanserai is a large, square building round an inner courtyard where, in this illustration, there are saddled camels. In this yard there is generally a covered well where leather water-bottles could be filled. This caravanserai has an arcade round the courtyard where the animals can shelter (*e*). A stone staircase (*d*) leads up to a first floor (*a*) of wooden beams on which are a number of small rooms available as lodgings for travellers. Mattresses for use as beds are hanging over the balustrade.

There is some difference of opinion concerning the inn mentioned in Luke 2: 7. I. Snoek, in his *Bethlehem en Nazareth* (pp. 149, 150), says: "The inn here is associated by some with the usual kind of eastern inn. According to them Joseph and Mary could not find room in the covered part, and so they had to find some place in the open courtyard." Most commentators reject this view. How are we then to visualize this inn in Luke 2: 7? There are three current explanations:

a. The inn was the property of Joseph himself, who came from Bethlehem, and during his absence it had been let to tenants. On his return to Bethlehem he would of course have found accommodation there, as it was his inn. When Mary's hour had come, they could no longer stay in the overcrowded house, and so they withdrew into that part of the house which was used as a stable.

b. Any house was an inn to a stranger if it would offer him a lodging. Luke 2: 7 refers to no more than an ordinary farmhouse. The *fellah's* home, as we have seen, was divided into two parts with the family's quarters on one level, and the animals' on a lower level. It was in this lower part that they would have made a room for Joseph and Mary. On either side of the few steps leading up were the mangers (plate 5, 2*c*); one of these might have been the crib. Both schools of thought emphasize that Luke 2: 6 says, "while they were there" and not "when they came there". Mary and Joseph must have been in Bethlehem for quite a time before the birth, and so their stay in a private house was only to be expected.

c. The traditional explanation: the birth took place in a cave used as a sheep-fold. It was not at all unusual for people to spend the night in animals' enclosures in Palestine. A warm shelter like that was a better place for Mary in her condition than the inn. If we adhere to tradition we can imagine the sequence of events as follows: Joseph and Mary come to Bethlehem. Everywhere is full up. There is no room at the inn either. They are directed to a cave used as a sheep-fold. This view is confirmed by the words of the angel telling the shepherds that they will find the little child in the manger, the manger they were familiar with, hence in the shelter to which they used to lead their flock. And Dalman agrees with this: "It may well be that age-old tradition has happened to hit upon the truth."

31. IMPLEMENTS OF WAR

1. Sea battle between the Egyptians and the Philistines. The archer on the right is Pharaoh Rameses (1198–1167). Over his short skirt he is wearing a long outer garment, only the bottom edge of which is indicated by a single line. In the bottom row, Philistines are being led away captive. Above them are three rows of ships, all of which have sails which are furled; but whereas the Egyptian ships have oars in addition, the Philistine ships depend on sail alone. The Philistines are armed with daggers and lances, which means that they can only fight in close combat. The preponderance of arrows on the right is intended by the artist to show that an Egyptian victory is assured.

2. Thothmes IV in battle. The king stands in all his majesty in his chariot drawn by two rearing stallions. Above his head is the goddess Nechbet (*a*) in the form of a vulture, with the king under the shadow of its wings. The king has a battle-axe (*b*) in one hand and a bow (*c*) in the other; he is carrying two quivers. There are bracelets on his upper arm and the reins are held round his waist. He is pursuing the fleeing Asiatics with their typical spade beards. Armed with bows and arrows and daggers, they are trying to defend themselves with their rectangular shields, but their "shields, bows, daggers" cannot save them.

3. Egyptian soldiers in the days of Rameses III (1198–1167). They are carrying lances, shields and swords. The Egyptian shield (*a*) is fairly long, with a straight bottom edge and rounded at the top. The soldiers are armed alternately with daggers and with sickle-shaped swords (*b*). Every fifth man (perhaps a "corporal") carries a baton. The Bible alludes to the burning of shields (e.g. Ezek. 39: 9), and to the anointing of shields (2 Sam. 1: 21; Isa. 21: 5), from which we might conclude that the shields of the Israelites, like those of other nations, were made of wood covered with leather or of several layers of leather alone. The sword and the lance belonged to the equipment of the heavily armed soldier.

4. Egyptian coat of mail. Originally the coat of mail did not form part of the equipment of the ordinary soldier but was worn by leading citizens only (Goliath, 1 Sam. 17: 5; Saul, 1 Sam. 31: 4; Ahab, 1 Kings 22: 34). Uzziah was the first to prepare coats of mail for the whole army (2 Chron. 26: 14). The coat of mail for the soldiers consisted of a leather jerkin covered with small metal plates.

5. Rameses II takes Ascalon. The town is surrounded with a double wall (*a, b*). The Egyptians are advancing, carrying oval shields (*c*). In the centre is the gate (*d*), and a soldier is setting about the wooden door with an axe (*e*). To the right and left are scaling ladders (*f*), one of which is being used by a soldier for his ascent, with a dagger in his hand and a shield on his back (*g*). The men on the upper walls are crying for mercy with hands raised, while one of them to the right is holding up a burning censer (*h*) as a token of submission. Another of the men on the right is lowering his child from the wall and on the left a man is lowering his wife.

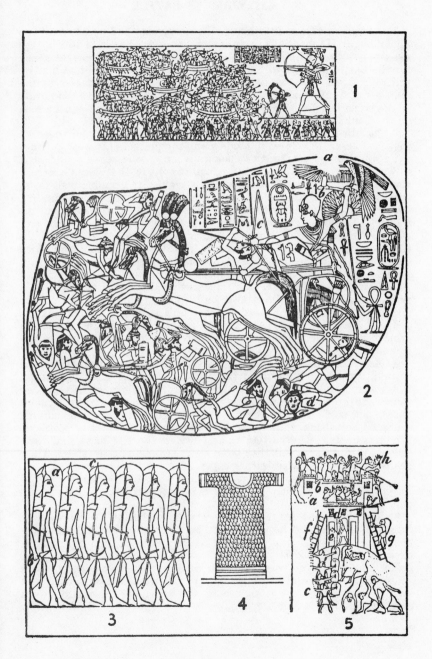

32. ASSYRIANS IN BATTLE

1. Assyrian battle in marshland. The Assyrians had no navy. When Shalmaneser III mentions in an inscription a sea battle in which "the sea was reddened with blood", he must have been grossly exaggerating, for the battle referred to took place on a small lake. Nor should we think in terms of a sea battle when Sennacherib waged war in the marshes of South Babylonia, where the Assyrians pursued the enemy in boats made from willow branches. Assyrian horsemen can be seen on the banks among the trees.

2. Tiglath-Pileser IV seizes Gezer. The doughty Assyrian monarch Tiglath-Pileser IV (745–727), made many conquests in the west (2 Kings 15: 29ff), and against Judah's enemies when, in the·year 734, he went to war at the request of Ahaz (2 Kings 16: 9). In that year Gezer was also captured as this relief shows. Up against the double wall (*a, a*) with its fortified towers (*b*) stands an Assyrian battering-ram (*c*), which has two rams (*d*) with metal points to break up the stones in the wall (*e*). A soldier is in the act of jumping from the ram onto the city wall, while behind him another soldier, armed with a dagger (*h*), is advancing under cover of a large screen (*f*) which he is holding, and which also shields an archer (*i*). The soldier storming the wall is armed with a round Assyrian shield (*j*) and a spear (*k*).

3. Assyrian standard. A disc representing the sun is mounted on a richly ornate shaft. Above two bulls that are moving in opposite directions is a triangle formed by the sun's rays, and above this the godhead Assur (*a*), who is shooting an arrow. His head and helmet (*b*) project above the rim of the disc thereby forming the apex of the standard.

4. Assyrian archers. The main body of the Assyrian army consisted of infantrymen, and of these the archers were the most important. Bows were made of wood, but also of horn. The arrows had wooden shafts and bronze or iron points, triangular in shape, with or without barbs. The soldiers were expert in archery, whether driving in chariots, riding on horseback, standing or kneeling, and in all kinds of positions. When marching they carried their bows in the left hand and their quivers in the right, and they wore short swords at their sides. Their heads were covered with leather caps.

5. Assyrian slinger. Slingers formed a special detachment in the Assyrian army, and they were called into action both in attack and defence.

6. Heavily armed Assyrian. This man is a chariot soldier, fighting from the chariot, and he wears a leather helmet with metal reinforcements (*a*), a coat of mail extending to his ankles (*b*), and a protective covering for his neck (*c*). His weapons are the spear (*d*) and sword (*e*). As in Israel the sword was straight (1 Sam. 31: 4ff), two-edged (Judges 3: 16; Prov. 5: 4) and short (Judges 3: 21ff); it was also carried in a leather sheath (1 Sam. 17: 51; 2 Sam. 20: 8) attached to a girdle worn over the uniform (1 Sam. 17: 39).

33. WEAPONS

1. Hittite. This warrior has a square beard but no moustache. His very long nose is a typical characteristic and his hair is plaited at the back of his neck (*a*). His high pointed cap (*b*) has a decorated rim which runs up to a point at the front and back (*c*). The upper part of the body is clothed in a shirt (*d*) over which is worn a skirt covering the hips and tied with a wide girdle. On his feet he wears shoes (*e*), pointed and turned up at the toes. His weapons are a sword (*f*), a long spear (*g*) and a Pontic shield (*h*).

2. Hittite war-chariot. It is generally thought that the war-chariot came to the Israelites from the Hittites (cf. 1 Kings 10: 29). There were three men in the chariot, the driver (*a*), the shield-bearer (*b*) and the actual warrior (*c*). (In Egyptian chariots, on the other hand, there were only two people.) The third man therefore was the most important; it is significant that the Hebrew word for captain (e.g. in 2 Kings 9: 25) is sometimes rendered by "third man".

3. Egyptian chariot (princes of the king's house and their chariots). The chariot was intended to take two people; sometimes, however, as in the second chariot illustrated, there were three, the driver and two others. But this was a rare occurrence, except in triumphal processions when the king was followed by two princes in their chariot.

4. Dagger and ceremonial sword at Shechem. *Fellahs* from Balâtah have discovered undamaged tombs at the foot of Mount Ebal, containing bronze objects, arms and jewellery. The most important find was a large sickle-shaped sword made of bronze inlaid with gold; a masterpiece showing the influence of Egyptian art. The technical term for this weapon is the Greek word *harpè*. Ceremonial swords similar to this have also been found in the tomb of the prince of Byblos (the biblical Gebal in Ezek. 27: 9). Although these swords were customarily buried with their royal owners, it is nevertheless remarkable that the first find at Shechem should have been such a show-piece (Professor Böhl). The handle is missing from the *harpè*. The dagger next to it is made of bronze.

5. Heavily armed Israelite with shield (*a*), spear (*b*) and helmet.

6. Lightly armed Israelite (from the same collection) with sling (*a*) and quiver (*b*).

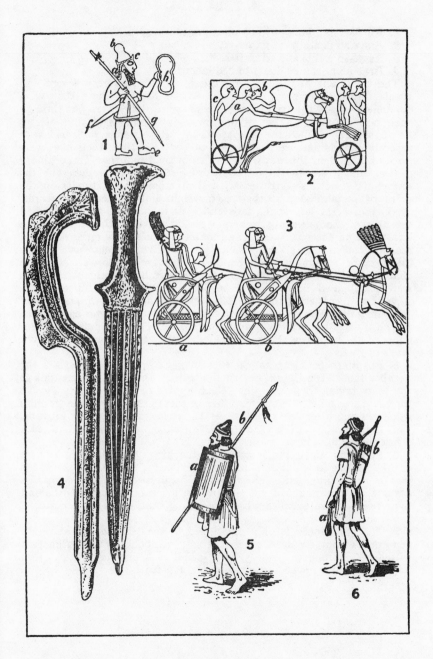

34. PRISONERS

1. **An Assyrian king putting out a prisoner's eyes.**
2. **Assyrian death penalty,** on poles.
3. **Assyrian ankle and wrist fetters.**
4. **Israelite prisoners doing forced labour.**

The treatment of prisoners by the Assyrians was very severe and cruel. Captured princes were taken to the capital where they were compelled to pull the triumphal royal chariot. Rings were put through their noses or lips, or they were thrown into kennels at the gate, to be abused and reviled by the passers-by. Rebels were punished very severely: hands and feet, noses and ears were cut off, their eyes were put out, and their tongues were torn from their mouths. The ordinary death penalty was by decapitation or hoisting on poles, whereby the unfortunate victims were tied with their stomachs or throats on the point of a stake so that their own weight pulled them downwards. Shalmaneser III left young lads and girls to burn in a town he had set ablaze. Sometimes prisoners were flayed and their skins were hung taut on the city wall. The inhabitants of enemy cities who had escaped the massacre were taken away captive into slavery: "They cast lots for her honourable men, and all her great men were bound in chains" (Nahum 3: 10). The men were fettered hand and foot. Women were not chained, but the rough soldiers escorting them amused themselves by "discovering their skirts and to see the shame of nakedness" (Nahum 3: 5). The prisoners were ganged for forced labour as is shown in the illustration (taken from a marble relief in the palace of Sennacherib). Clothed in short skirted garments, they are carrying heavy loads of rocks.

5. **Egyptians counting hands from enemy corpses.** To ascertain the number killed, the Egyptians used to cut off the hands or genitals of the dead, taking them and piling them up in front of the king. Twelve thousand five hundred and thirty-five of these gruesome battle trophies were counted after one of Rameses III's victories over the Libyans. This is reminiscent of the story of David who was instructed to fetch a hundred Philistine foreskins (1 Sam. 18: 25).

6. **Prisoners under the footstool of the king.** The drawing is part of a larger one in which Amenhotep II (Pharaoh, 1448–1420) places his feet on the subjugated Negroes (*a*) and Semites (*b*) who are caught in a snare. The vanquished persons, whose arms have been tied behind their backs, were enemies who "have now been made his footstool" (Ps. 110: 1).

7. **The "footstool"** is only mentioned in the Bible as an attribute of princes sitting on the throne; it is used symbolically in conjunction with God's throne (Ps. 99: 5) and Isaiah in a prophetic description (ch. 66: 1) names even the earth as His footstool.

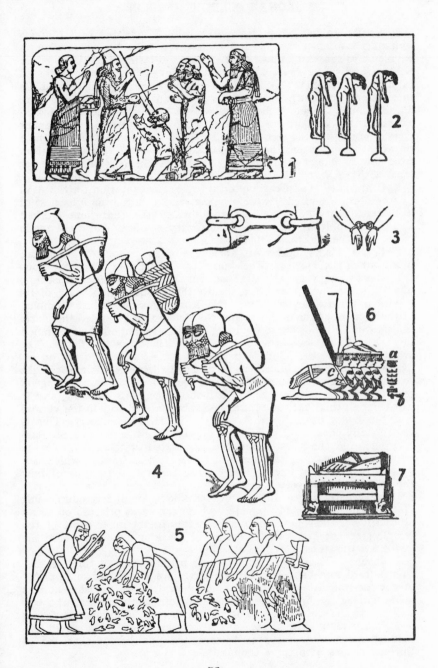

1. Roman soldier. The dress of a soldier consisted of (1) *tunica militaris*, a woollen shirt with short sleeves, (2) a *sagum, sagulum,* a woollen cloak reaching down to the knees and fastened on the shoulder with a clasp, (3) a *cingulum militare*, a belt (*a*). His equipment included (4) an infantry helmet (*b*), and (5) a *scutum*, an oblong shield (*c*) made of wood, covered with leather and metal, and carried on the left arm. In addition a soldier of the legion wore a harness of metal plates on his chest and back or, in some cases, a kind of hauberk. His weapons were: the *gladius*, the short, straight, two-edged sword (*d*) with which he would thrust rather than slash, and this he carried on a belt either from the shoulder or round the waist; the javelin (*e*) (*pilum*), six feet long, with a pointed spearhead of flexible metal.

2. Centurion (from a carving on a tomb). A centurion (in the A.V. "captain of a hundred") wore a helmet and a more ornate harness of a better quality. By courage and loyalty the centurions worked their way up from the ranks of ordinary soldiers, and were made officers by the general.

3. Carcer Mamertinus. An ancient Roman prison, "a dungeon, hewn out of the Tarpeian Rock near the Capitol, which has notorious associations from very early times not only because of political prisoners, like Jugurtha, who starved to death there, but also because of its fearful impenetrable seclusion. The Roman writer Sallust trembled at the thought of the darkness and the stench that pervaded the place. Today it is still possible to go down into this lugubrious hole hemmed in with walls cut out of solid basalt (*a*). There are two floors. The sweating face of the low, black vault bears menacingly down on us. There is not a single chink that would have allowed a glimmer of light to filter through. A round hole (*b*) in the floor of the upper dungeon provided the only access to the half-submerged prison below, and it was through this that the condemned were lowered to join the vermin and the bones of their predecessors" (B. H. Molkenboer). This is traditionally considered to be the dungeon for St. Peter and St. Paul in Rome, and the apostles are commemorated in the relief. To the left of this relief are instruments of torture (*c*), in front of which is a well (*d*) supplied by spring water. The inscription (*e*) tells of how the jailers were converted.

In very early times, in ancient Jerusalem, an underground vault (Jer. 37: 16) or a muddy pit (Jer. 38: 6) served as prisons; or, as an alternative, a room near the northern gate of the inner court of the temple (Jer. 20: 2), or the forecourt of the king's palace, where the guard was quartered (Jer. 32: 2).

4. Scourge. The Roman scourge was made of two or three leather thongs fixed to a handle and terminating in a number of small pieces of zinc or iron attached to them at intervals. The punishment was made harsher by dint of the stooping attitude of the victim, who was stripped to the waist. According to Jewish law the number of stripes was forty minus one (Deut. 25: 3), either in order to avoid exceeding the number forty or because the punishment consisted of thirteen stripes with three thongs (hence 13 x 3).

1, 2, 3. Tombs. It was considered an honour among the Israelites to be buried in a family tomb (Gen. 49: 31; 1 Kings 13: 22). Separate chambers were hewn out inside the tombs, of which there were three kinds: (1) Arched recess, a bench (b) under an arch (a) cut out of the rock face; at one end there is a slight rise (c), as a head-rest for the deceased. The body was laid unprotected by any covering on this shelf, so that it was less perfectly preserved than it would have been in a sarcophagus. (2) Arcosolium. A recess was first cut in the rock face above ground level, and this enabled a trough to be cut out of the rock shelf so formed (a) about the length of a man, thus hewing out an arcosolium similar to a stone coffin. If, moreover, the recess was given an arched ceiling (as for the arched recess), we have a type of grave common in catacombs. (3) Shaft grave or kokim. Deep, narrow compartments were hewn out running in at right angles to the rock face. The bodies were pushed into these recesses head first. The narrow width enabled the shaft to be shut off with a flat stone. These three kinds of grave all existed in sepulchral chambers. Access to these was obtained through

4. The entrance hall of the chamber. This ante-chamber is as wide as the tomb chamber itself (as is clear from plate No. 5), but the doorway beyond is very small, so that one has to stoop to enter the sepulchre (Luke 24: 12; John 20: 11). In front of this entrance there was often a groove or rut to take a stone, which was rolled in front of the doorway (Mark 16: 3) and was sometimes round (as at 5c).

5. This model of a sepulchre with entrance hall shows clearly the hall (a), the entrance of the sepulchre (b) and the stone (c). A study of what the Gospels tell us about Jesus' grave yields the following information. The sepulchre was approached through the entrance hall (John 20: 1, 3, 5, 6, 8). Presumably the tomb had an open entrance hall. Then those who came to the tomb had to stoop in order to look inside (Luke 24: 12; John 20: 11), which confirms that the entrance was low. They could then see straight into the sepulchre so that there cannot have been a forecourt between the entrance hall and the tomb chamber containing the graves. To the right there was a seat (Mark 16: 5), and the angels sat one at the head and one at the feet of the place where the body of Jesus had lain (John 20: 12); so this cannot have been a shaft grave. It is not stated that the disciples found the tomb empty when they looked inside (which would have been immediately apparent in the case of an arched recess) but that they discovered the linen clothes (Luke 24: 12; John 20: 7); so it was presumably an arcosolium. Now in the vicinity of Jerusalem are situated the tombs of the kings of the royal family of Adiabene dating from the first century, and from these we learn what the tombs of the wealthy were like (cf. Isa. 53: 9). We can thus deduce that the arched recess and the arcosolium were the normal forms at that time in Jerusalem, and we can assume that the wealthy Joseph of Arimathea (Matt. 27: 57), who was a counsellor (Mark 15: 43), had a grave made that was the best possible in his day, that is to say an arcosolium.

37. MOURNING

1. **Egyptian relief illustrating part of a scene at a burial,** in a tomb belonging to an official of about 1350 B.C. A group of mourning women at their lamentations is shown. The Bible too mentions them, "call for the mourning women, that they may come" (Jer. 9: 17) and, "they shall call the husbandmen to mourning, and such as are skilful of lamentation to wailing" (Amos 5: 16). These lamentations were accompanied on the flute. The woman in the centre (*a*) is wearing a cloth round her hips. In Israel this was called the sack, a cloth worn round the bare hips when lamenting a dead person (Jacob put sack-cloth round his loins when he thought that Joseph was dead, Gen. 37: 34, cf. 2 Sam. 3: 31); sackcloth was also worn as a sign of sadness (1 Kings 20: 31) and mortification (Matt. 11: 21).

2. **Sarcophagus of King Ahiram of Byblos** (city in Syria, the biblical Gebal, Ezek. 27: 9). The coffin rests on four recumbent lions. The relief shows the king on the left with a table in front of him, to which men are coming with gifts for him (cf. Ps. 72: 10). Along the upper edge is an inscription in Phoenician characters.

For the sake of comparison, the same inscription is also given in Hebrew square script, the translation of which is:

Sarcophagus which (Itto)baal, son of Ahiram, king of Gebal, made for Ahiram.

Outside Palestine, burial in coffins was customary only among those of high rank (Gen. 50: 26); in Israel people were probably buried in their ordinary clothes, according to the evidence in 1 Samuel 28: 14.

3. **Egyptian representation of mourning women.** In times of mourning and sorrow people sprinkled ash on their heads (Joshua 7: 6), and in wailing, the hand was placed on the head. The prophet says to Israel while under punishment, "Thou shalt go forth from him and thine hands upon thine head" (Jer. 2: 37). "And Tamar put ashes on her head, and rent her garment of divers colours that was on her, and laid her hand on her head, and went on crying" (2 Sam. 13: 19).

ארן זפעל [ואת]בעל בן אחרם מלך גבל לאחרם

38. TREES (1)

1. Felling of cedars in the Lebanon. Pharaoh Sethos I had commanded the felling of trees in the Lebanon, in order to make a barque (Nile ship) for the temple of Amon. "The great princes of the Lebanon" are wearing long cloaks and tippets. The trees depicted must be cedars; they were felled close to the ground with axes and were pulled over with ropes.

2. Assyrian soldiers felling trees. When Shalmaneser in his war against Hazaèl forced the Syrian king to retreat, but failed to take the city of Damascus, he vented his wrath by having the palms around the town (then as now) cut down. He laid waste the entire region as far as Hauran. There is a similar illustration of Sennacherib's soldiers felling palms with axes (*a*). The fruit (*b*) can be seen hanging under crowns of leaves. A canal (*c*) containing fish flows past the palm grove. The felling of fruit trees during a siege was prohibited by law in Israel (Deut. 20: 19), but the Israelites certainly found to their loss that their enemies did it (Isa. 14: 8).

3. Terebinth. The terebinth or turpentine tree (called "oak" in the A.V.) is one of the finest trees in Palestine. As a rule it stands all by itself and so attracts immediate attention. The dense foliage throws a dark shadow in the summer. Hosea 4: 13 refers to the terebinth as a tree "the shadow whereof is good"; it only casts this shadow in the summer, for this is the tree of which Isaiah (1: 30) says "whose leaf fadeth". Its huge crown and dense shadow impressed people in ancient times. "Only a man who has come from the stillness of the great desert is aware of the number of voices in a tree" (G. A. Smith). There are ten places in the Old Testament where idolatry "under every green tree" (Deut. 12: 2, the first of the references) is deprecated. Israel too fell under the enchantment: "she is gone up upon every high mountain and under every green tree, and there has played the harlot" (Jer. 3: 6). Idolatry was practised in the shade of the terebinth, so that the prophet declares in the Lord's name: "They shall learn that I am the Eternal, when their slain men lie among their idols around about their altars, at every shrine on the top of every hill and under every green tree and below every leafy terebinth, where they used to offer fragrant smoke to their idols" (Ezek. 6: 13, Moffatt). The terebinth was also regarded as a sacred tree by the Israelites: the "oak which was by Shechem" (Gen. 35: 4. See also Joshua 24: 26), the "oak which is at Ophrah" (Judges 6: 11), and in Jabesh (1 Chron. 10: 12), all these are terebinths. In the valley of Elah (1 Sam. 17: 2, Elah = terebinth) there were terebinths.

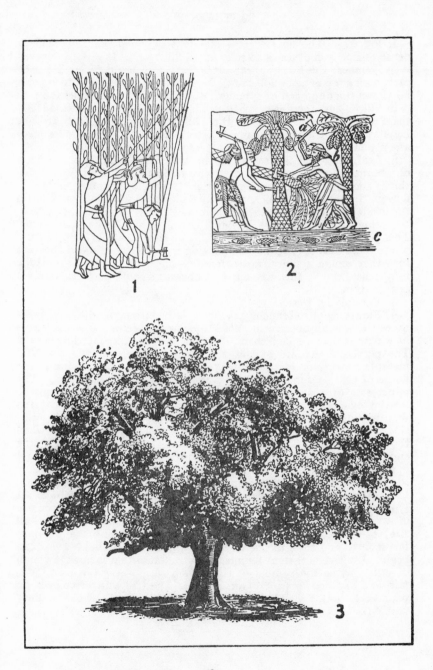

39. TREES (2)

1. Fig tree. The fig tree is a stately tree under whose spread of dense foliage it is pleasant to relax (cf. John 1: 48). It sheds its leaves in November; the buds appear in January and begin to swell in the early spring (cf. Song of Sol. 2: 13); in March the leaves begin to appear, heralding the approach of summer (Matt. 24: 32). As soon as the tree is in full foliage, there is early fruit which is eaten unripe (Isa. 28: 4); these were lacking, however, on the "withered fig tree" (Matt. 21: 19). By May, when the young summer figs are visible, the early ones have already fallen (Nahum 3: 12; Rev. 6: 13).

2. Leaf, fruit and flowers of the fig tree. The drawing shows part of a branch of the common fig tree with its leaves and fruit (*a*). Under this is shown the false fruit in section (*b*), a male (*c*) and a female (*d*) flower. In these trees the monosexual flowers grow side by side on the inside of a hollow torus which sprouts straight out from the branch, becoming larger and more bulbous, acquiring finally its pear shape. This pericarp is the edible fig, though in fact the true fruit consists of the seeds inside. The leaves of the fig tree are thick, and if they are torn they exude a slimy sap with which one leaf can easily be stuck to another, and in this way our first ancestors could make themselves aprons (Gen. 3: 7).

3. Very old fig tree.

4. Flowering olive branch. Like many other trees round the Mediterranean this is an evergreen. Yet although it does not shed its leaves in winter it does replace them all in the course of about three years. The perpetual verdure of this tree accounts then for the beautiful metaphor in Psalm 52: 1, "but like an olive green am I, living in the house of God" (Moffatt). The leaves resemble willow leaves (*a*). The upper side of a dull green colour has a thick leathery epidermis to restrict evaporation. For the same reason the underside is covered with minute stars of fine hairs (deformed epidermis cells), giving this side a whitish appearance. In Palestine early May is the time when the olive tree is in flower. Then in the axles of the leaves and at the ends of the young branches short trusses of small white flowers (*b*) appear, having little or no scent. After pollination by insects, they soon begin to form fruit. Sometimes, however, when no pollination takes place, all the flowers are shed before the fruit has begun to set (Job 15: 33). The fruit is a stone fruit with the shape and structure of a pointed plum. By September the olives have acquired their full size; the oil content too has greatly increased during the previous few months and towards the middle of October the actual harvest can begin. The tree is then at its most beautiful, and that is how Jeremiah describes it, as the symbol of the chosen race: "A green olive tree, fair, and of a goodly fruit" (Jer. 11: 16). The tree will thrive even on poor, rocky soil, and this justifies the description "oil out of the flinty rock" (Deut. 32: 13).

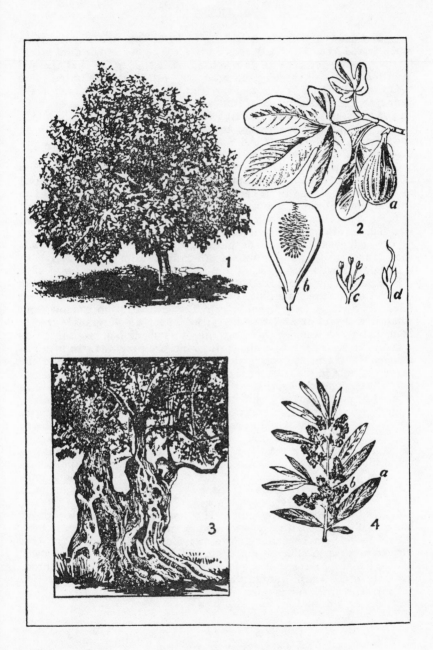

40. TREES (3)

1. The date palm has a height of 30 to 60 feet and sometimes as much as 160 feet. The trunk runs up to a crown of 40 to 60 dark green, feathery leaves, sometimes as much as ten feet long, so that there is good reason to call them "palm branches" (*a*). It is usually ten years before a date palm begins to bear fruit, and then it will bear every year from six to ten trusses of fruit, each containing hundreds of dates. In the olden days Jericho was rightly named "the city of palm trees" (Deut. 34: 3). Palms were also to be found in the oasis of Engedi on the western shore of the Dead Sea. Engedi was also called Hazezon-Tamar (Gen. 14: 7), which means the place of the cutting of palms.

The tree is the symbol of the righteous (Ps. 92: 13). At the institution of the Feast of Tabernacles (Lev. 23: 40), palm leaves were prescribed as part of the foliage to be carried by those appearing joyfully before the presence of the Lord, and apparently the palm leaf was a very important part since the bunch of green branches, the *lūlābh* in Hebrew, was named after it. Palm branches were symbolic of victory (Rev. 7: 9), and when Christ made his entry into Jerusalem, the crowds took branches of palm and went forth to meet Him (John 12: 13).

2. Pomegranate tree.

3. Branch, flower and fruit of the pomegranate. Wherever the Bible names the principal trees and fruits, the pomegranate is among them (Deut. 8: 8; Hag. 2: 19; Joel 1: 12). The tree casts no shadow, and when it was said of Saul that he tarried under a pomegranate tree (1 Sam. 14: 2), he was not there because of its shade but because it was a sacred tree. By the time the spring rains are over, the tree is in full foliage. It was in the spring that the bridegroom went out into the garden of nuts to see whether the pomegranates were budding (Song of Sol. 6: 11). The pomegranate is a dark red fruit ("thy temples are as a piece of pomegranate within thy locks", Song of Sol. 6: 7); to the bride "the juice of my pomegranate" is something delicious (Song of Sol. 8: 2). In shape it is like an apple, although it is really a berry bursting open when ripe, revealing its flesh and dark red, juicy pips (Song of Sol. 4: 3). From the juice of the fruit, pomegranate wine was made (Song of Sol. 8: 2), and because of their handsome shape, pomegranates provided the model for the decorations round the bronze chapiters in Solomon's temple (1 Kings 7: 18, 42; Jer. 52: 22, 23) and along the hem of the High Priest's robe (Exod. 28: 33, 34).

4. Wild fig tree or sycamore. The branches of this tree spread horizontally close to the ground, and so it is an easy tree to climb (Luke 19: 4); its beautiful foliage provides ample shade. The tree thrives in a warm climate, not up in the mountains but in the lower plains, "wild fig trees that are in the vale" (1 Kings 10: 27; 1 Chron. 27: 28), in the warm Jordan valley (Luke 19: 4) and in Egypt (Ps. 78: 47). The small fruit is eaten (Amos 7: 14).

41. TREES AND BUSHES (4)

1. St. John's bread tree (so called because it was thought, though with no certainty, that John the Baptist ate the fruit) is a tree not unlike an enlarged combination of two common shrubs, the acacia and the broom. It derives its Latin name, *ceratonia*, from the shape of the somewhat horny pods. The small beans in the black pods were at one time used as weights, called carats from the Greek word *keration*. Jewellers still use this word as a standard for gold and diamonds. Professor van Veldhuizen adds to his comments, from which the above notes on the bean are taken, this observation about the prodigal son: "according to St. Luke 15: 16, 'he would fain have filled his belly with the husks that the swine did eat, and no man gave unto him'. The question arises, why did he then not take some? To which the answer is that there was a famine in the land, and the swine had to find their own food while he tended them. In the evening they were given a feed, while he had to stand by looking on. It was more important to the owners that the swine should be well fed than that he was underfed. What was translated as husks were the *keration*, the fruit of the carob."

2. Branches of the almond tree: fruit (*a*), blossom (*b*). The almond tree flowers very early in the year; the buds appear in January, and in February the blossom is out, a wonderful sight at a time when snow is still in the air. Jeremiah (1: 11) once saw "a rod of an almond tree" (*maqqel saqed*), an almond branch, and he was to learn from this that God is wakeful over His word to carry it out (Jer. 11: 12, Moffatt). Indeed, the almond tree never seems to be asleep (and Moffatt translates: "The shoot of a wake-tree"), and for that reason it is a fitting symbol in the vision. The fact that Aaron's rod burst into flower during one night (Num. 17: 8) has something to do with its being an almond branch. The flowers are first flushed with red, becoming entirely white, and are therefore a symbol of old age (Eccles. 12: 5). The almond was considered one of the best fruits in the land (Gen. 43: 11) and it served as a motif for decorating the golden candlestick (Exod. 25: 33, 34; 37: 19).

3. Myrrh. The resin of this plant was greatly valued. Myrrh was a component of the holy anointing oil (the purest myrrh, sweet cinnamon, calamus, cassia, olive oil, Exod. 30: 23), because of its delicate scent ("my fingers dripped with sweet smelling myrrh", Song of Sol. 5: 5). It was used as a perfume for scenting clothes (Ps. 45: 8 "all thy garments smell of myrrh, aloes and cassia"; cf. Song of Sol. 3: 6) and for beds (Prov. 7: 17). "Oil of myrrh" was a beauty preparation (Esther 2: 12). It was often carried in chains or sweet balls (Isa. 3: 19), or bundles of myrrh were worn on the breast (Song of Sol. 1: 13). The gifts of the wise men from the east consisted of gold, frankincense and myrrh (Matt. 2: 11); Nicodemus brought a mixture of myrrh and aloes for Jesus' burial (John 19: 39). Myrrh was also mixed with the wine at the Cross (Mark 15: 23).

4. Nard. The root of this plant yields the spikenard preserved in alabaster boxes (Mark 14: 3; John 12: 3). In deducing from the Song of Solomon 1: 12; 4: 13, 14 that nard was grown in the gardens of Palestine, we ought rather to interpret this plant as a kind of valerian. It is however often difficult to be sure about the plants named in the Bible.

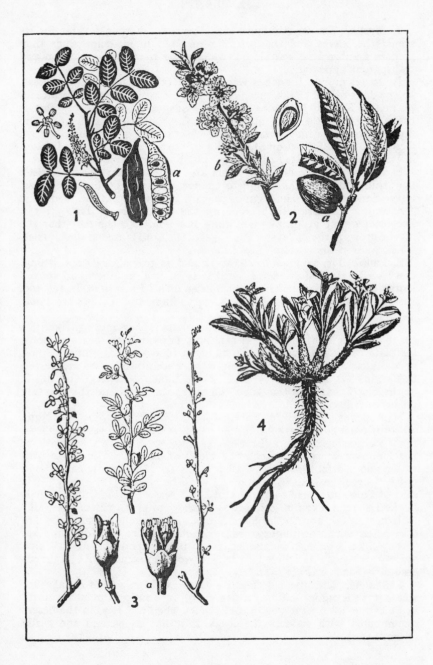

42. PLANTS

1. Myrtle. The myrtle has always been much sought after for its scent; the leaves and the berries were used in medicine since they contain an aromatic, volatile oil (which gives the leaves a mottled and transparent appearance).

In Israel myrtle branches were used at the Feast of Tabernacles. In the days of Nehemiah there was a wooded region west of Jerusalem (the name Kirjath-Jearim = town of woods, cf. Joshua 15: 9), whence branches of myrtle were fetched to make booths (Neh. 8: 16). The myrtle grows in valleys where the soil has plenty of moisture, so that a complete transformation of desert soil into a watery region is implied in Isaiah's prophecy (41: 19) "I shall plant a myrtle tree in the desert". When those that are heavy of heart are invited to partake of Christ's bountiful goodness, the complete change that will be brought about in the dark world by His reign of peace is summed up in the prediction "instead of the briar shall come up the myrtle tree" (Isa. 55: 13). Zechariah's first vision at night time also points to the fact that the myrtle grows in the valleys: "The angel of the Lord is among the myrtles, which were in the bottom" (Zech. 1: 8–11).

2. Lentil. The common lentil, an annual, is grown for its nourishing, tasty seeds. In Palestine the lentil is sown in December, and cooked lentils are very popular as a hot winter dish. In ancient Israel, too, the lentil was well known (Gen. 25: 34; 2 Sam. 17: 28; 23: 11; Ezek. 4: 9).

3. Hyssop. The plant shown in the plate is *hyssopus officinalis*, a shrub with a profusion of stems, and flowers with pentapetalous, bilabiate calyx (*a*) usually surrounding a blue and sometimes a pink or white crown. The use of hyssop in holy scripture is first mentioned in Exodus 12: 22, "And ye shall take a bunch of hyssop and dip it in the blood that is in the basin and strike the lintel and the two side posts".

Hyssop was also used for water of separation (purification) (cf. Num. 19: 6) while a combination of cedar wood, scarlet and hyssop was used for the cleansing of lepers (Lev. 14: 4, 6, 49, 51, 52). In the Epistle to the Hebrews 9: 19: "he took the blood of calves and of goats with water and scarlet wool and hyssop" and for the same reason David cried "purge me with hyssop, and I shall be clean" (Ps. 51: 7). It is said of Solomon: "He also spake of the trees, from the cedar, that is in the Lebanon, even unto the hyssop, that springeth out of the wall" (1 Kings 4: 33), and so the hyssop, one of the smallest plants, is here contrasted with the mighty cedar. And lastly in St. John 19: 29, "They filled a sponge with vinegar and put it upon hyssop". Which variety of hyssop is alluded to here is open to some doubt; Linneus assumed that it was the *hyssopus officinalis*.

4. Shalots. The shalot derives its name from the city of Ascalon (of which it is the onion—*allium ascalonicum*). It is still a popular favourite in Palestine, even as it was in early times when the Jews in the desert remembered with sadness the leeks and the onions and the garlic (Num. 11: 5).

43. ANIMALS (1)

1. Dromedary. 2. Camel. In Hebrew there is no distinction between camel and dromedary. Even in later times, when mention is made in prophecies of camels in Babel (Isa. 21: 7), in the south country (Isa. 30: 6), and with the Arabs (Jer. 49: 29, 32), the one word *gāmāl* is always used. So there was apparently no characteristic difference in the eyes of the Israelites between camels with one or two humps, yet there is evidence that they were not unobservant about camels in the separate words they used for the male and the female foals. Hence the A.V. translation of Isaiah 60: 6 "the multitude of camels shall cover thee" refers to the Hebrew *bĕkher*, meaning young male camels, while in Jeremiah 2: 23 "thou art a swift dromedary traversing her ways" the original has the word *bikhrā* for a female foal (F. J. Bruijel).

3. The gazelle is still extant in Palestine. The animal is admired for its speed, cf. 2 Samuel 2: 18, where Asahel is described as "light of foot as a wild roe" (See also 1 Chron. 12: 8; Song of Sol. 2: 17 and Isa. 13: 14). "Then, like hunted gazelles, like sheep unshepherded, shall men be hurrying home, each off to his own land" (Moffatt). In Song of Solomon (2: 7; 4: 5) the gazelle typifies gracefulness. The name Zibiah (for a man, 1 Chron. 8: 9 and for a woman, 2 Kings 12: 1) and Dorcas (Acts 9: 36) indicate that the name "gazelle" was given to humans. The law allowed its meat to be eaten (Deut. 14: 5) and so it was hunted (1 Kings 4: 23). But it was not used for sacrifices (Deut. 12: 5).

4. The ibex with its powerful horns used to be common in the mountainous regions of Palestine (cf. 1 Sam. 24: 2, "the rocks of the wild goats" near Engedi; and in Ps. 104: 18, "the high hills are a refuge for the wild goats"). They are still to be found among the rocks round the Dead Sea, also mentioned by Job (Job 39: 1, "the wild goats of the rock"). The female of the ibex was admired by the Arabs for its speed and gracefulness, while in Proverbs the wife of youth is called "a pleasant roe" (Prov. 5: 19).

5. The onager is called a wild ass in the Authorized Version. "It is of the same size as the tame donkey, but its legs are more delicate. It has a slender neck, slightly curved, and long, upright ears. The mane is dark, whereas the body is of a light colour. A brown, bristly ridge runs from the mane to the tail" (F. J. Bruijel). They live wild in the plains (cf. Job 39: 5-9); the freedom-loving peoples of Ishmael's offspring are compared to them (Gen. 16: 12). They live in the wilderness and eat grass (Job 6: 5), the open country is their home (Job 39: 5, 6). So the judgement of destruction is exactly as Isaiah prophesied, "the forts and towers shall be for dens for ever, a joy of wild asses, a pasture of flocks" (Isa. 32: 14). The wild asses, accustomed to the wilderness (Jer. 2: 24; Job 24: 5) also move to the bare mountains, where they drink water from the springs in the valleys (Ps. 104: 11).

44. ANIMALS (2)

1. The mule is a cross between a he-ass and a mare (Esther 8: 10). It is strong and brave like a horse, with the cautious tread of a donkey (Esther 8: 14). During the time of David, the mule was ridden by princes (2 Sam. 13: 29; 2 Sam. 18: 9). It makes an excellent pack animal (1 Chron. 12: 40); Naaman, for example, wanted to take earth from Israel, "two mules' burden of earth" (2 Kings 5: 17), and it was also used in the army (Zech. 14: 15). Crossbreeding was prohibited by law (Lev. 19: 19) so these animals were probably purchased elsewhere; the people of Togarmah possessed mule studs, as we learn from Ezekiel 27: 14: "they of the House of Togarmah traded in thy fairs with horses and horsemen and mules".

2. The goat. Its ears were long and floppy. A shepherd when wrestling with a lion might perhaps be able to rescue a piece of his goat's ear (Amos 3: 12). The goats had long, black hair (Song of Sol. 4: 1; 6: 5), hence the black tents made of goat's hair (Song of Sol. 1: 5), and the resemblance of a goatskin to David's hair (1 Sam. 19: 13). The meat provided a favourite savoury dish (Gen. 27: 9; Luke 15: 29; Judges 6: 19; 13: 15; 15: 1; 1 Sam. 16: 20). To have sufficient goat's milk was regarded as a blessing (Prov. 27: 27). The goatskin was used for water bottles, sometimes even as a poor man's raiment (Heb. 11: 37). The goat's hair was spun by women into cloth (Exod. 35: 26) for tent coverings (Exod 26: 7). The flocks of goats generally grazed on mountains or hills, hence the description in 1 Kings 20: 27 of the Israelite army "like two little flocks of kids".

3. The fat-tailed sheep is to be recognized by its fat, fleshy tail. It was stipulated that in making an offering, the sacrificer should "take the whole rump, it shall be taken off hard by the back bone" (Lev. 3: 9). The colour of the wool is normally white (Ps. 147: 16; Isa. 1: 18; Dan. 7: 9; Rev. 1: 14; Song of Sol. 6: 6), with brown, sometimes black, legs and head; this explains the compact between Jacob and Laban (Gen. 30: 32). The sheep were described as by nature kind-hearted, not wilful, fearful, defenceless, patient in suffering (Isa. 53: 6, 7; Jer. 11: 19; Ps. 119: 176). The sheep was useful in Israel because of its milk (Deut. 32: 14; Isa. 7: 21, 22), the meat (1 Sam. 25: 18; 2 Sam. 12: 4; 1 Kings 4: 23) and the wool, which was woven into cloth (Job 31: 19, 20).

4. The hyrax, a small animal, lives in large companies in rocky areas ("the rocks are a refuge for the conies" Ps. 104: 18). In the Authorized Version the Hebrew word is translated by coney (Prov. 30: 26; Lev. 11: 35; Deut. 40: 7). If now the biblical coney is replaced by the hyrax, we find that the writer is not far wrong in saying that this animal "cheweth the cud, but divideth not the hoof" (Lev. 11: 5).

5. Quail. Every year the quails migrate in huge flocks; when they are exhausted they fall to the earth and are often picked up by the Arabs to be eaten as a delicacy, just as they were for the ancient Israelites on their journey through the wilderness (Exod. 16: 13; Num. 11: 31; Ps. 105: 40).

45. LOCUST, ANTS AND GECKO

1. Winged migratory locust. 2. Migratory locust in the final stage of its development. Damage is primarily caused by the migratory locusts which at certain times swoop down in enormous numbers. For this reason the innumerable hosts of an army, like that of the Midianites are described "as grasshoppers for multitude" (Judges 6: 5) and the armies that overpower Egypt are "more than the grasshoppers, and are innumerable" (Jer. 46: 23). "The locusts have no king to lead them", yet although they move in enormous swarms, "they advance in order" (Prov. 30: 27, Moffatt).

> They charge like warriors, they advance like fighters,
> each on his own track—no tangling of paths—
> none pushes his fellow, each follows his own line;
> they burst through weapons unbroken,
> they rush on the city, run over the walls,
> climb into the houses and enter the windows like thieves.
>
> (Joel 2: 7–9, Moffatt)

Terrible is the destruction: "the land is as the garden of Eden before them, and behind them a desolate wilderness; yea, and nothing shall escape them" (Joel 2: 3). Locusts are often symbolic of God's judgement from on high (Deut. 28: 38; Amos 4: 9; Amos 7: 1, "the locust spoiled your fig trees and your vines"). They are borne forward on the south-east wind in Palestine (Joel 2: 20; Ps. 109: 23). In Joel 1: 4:

> What the lopping locust left,
> the swarming locust ate,
> what the swarming locust left,
> the leaping locust ate,
> and what the leaping locust left,
> the devouring locust ate. (Moffatt)

The four names used in the Hebrew probably denote the four stages in the insect's development.

3. Ants: male (3*b*); female (3*a*); worker (3*c*), enlarged on the left, life size on the right. There are thirty-one types of ants in Palestine. The writer of Proverbs quotes the ants as examples of diligence, for the ant "provideth her meat in the summer and gathereth her food in the harvest" (Prov. 6: 8). "They prepare their meat in the summer" (Prov. 30: 25); the kinds of ant that live on plant foods and in particular on seeds from plants cannot find enough in the winter and must therefore lay in a store during the summer.

4. Gecko. The Authorized Version of Proverbs 30: 28 reads: "The spider taketh hold with her hands and is in king's palaces", but Moffatt's version is: "The lizard—you may lift it in your hand, but it will push into a palace." We should take the lizard here to mean the gecko, which does come into the house. Bruijel comments on this animal: "On the underside of their elongated toes they have suction pads enabling them to walk on walls in all directions." Dr. Gemser adds to this: "The lizard which runs so silently up the wall in search of food can quite safely be caught in the hand. Insignificant though it is, it can find a way into places to which few people would be allowed to gain access."

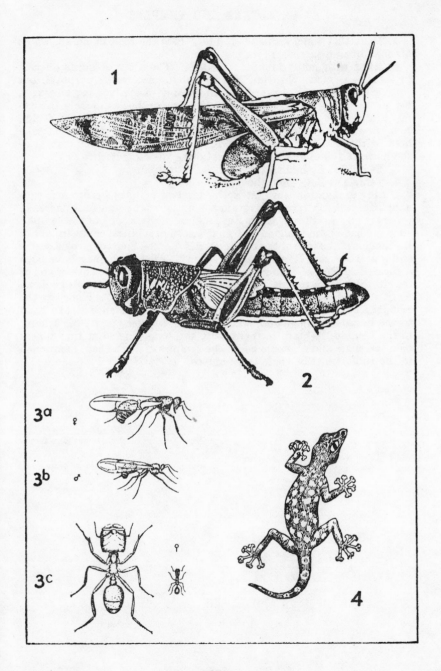

46. ALTARS AND TEMPLES

1. Rock that could serve as an altar. It is the rock at Zorah, where Manoah offered sacrifices (Judges 13: 19).

2. Altar with horns found at Megiddo. The altar of burnt offering in Israel was made with four horns, not for decorative purposes, but to be covered by the blood of the sin offering (Exod. 29: 12; Lev. 4: 7, 25, 30, 34; 8: 15; 9: 9; 16: 18). The horns were thus a symbol of atonement, and hence Christ is called a "horn of salvation" (Luke 1: 69). A man who had unintentionally committed manslaughter could take hold of the horns of the altar (1 Kings 1: 50; 2: 28). Desecration of the horns of the altar meant desecration of the altar itself.

3. Temple at Beth-shan (house of Ashtaroth).

4. Temple at Beth-shan (house of Dagon).

During excavation work, at Beth-shan two temples were found, running from east to west in a stratum belonging to the time of Rameses II (1292–1225). According to an Egyptian inscription, one of the temples seems to have been founded by "an overlord of soldiers, commandant of the archers of the lord of the two countries (i.e. the Pharaoh), royal scribe and grand overseer Ramses-uesr-chepesh". The temple may have been dedicated to Reshef, who was none other than Mekal, the ancient god of the city. The other temple, however, was dedicated to the female godhead Antit, "the queen of heaven, the mistress of all gods". Since, on the evidence of 1 Chronicles 10: 10, the Philistines fastened Saul's head to the house of Dagon, and, according to 1 Samuel 31: 10, his armour in the house of Ashtaroth, there must still have existed at that time a cult of a male and a female god. The temples of Beth-shan, mentioned in the Bible, must be these two temples.

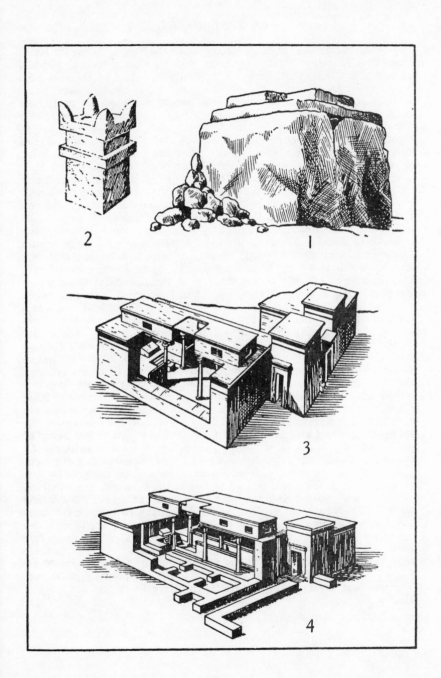

2

1

3

4

47. TABERNACLE

The tabernacle and the court (according to the Rev. L. Schouten Hzn).
The court (Exod. 27: 9–18; 38: 9–20) was an open rectangular space.
It was a hundred cubits long and fifty cubits wide, and the enclosure
was formed by hangings of fine linen suspended from pillars. There
were twenty pillars on the south side, and as many on the north, ten
on the west and ten on the east. In each of the four corners were two
pillars (E). On the east or front side, in the centre, was a screen,
"gate", hung from four pillars (Exod. 27: 16). The hangings were of
fine, twined linen of a pure white. They hung from silver hooks in
silver fillets fixed under the silver chapiters of the pillars, and they
had a height of five cubits (Exod. 27: 18). In the centre of the east side
of the enclosure of the court was a hanging called the gate (Exod.
27: 16) through which one entered the court, and during the ceremony
the hanging was either gathered up or pushed aside.

In the court is first and foremost the altar (B), a description of which
is given in Exodus 27: 1–8; 38: 1–7. It consisted of a large square
frame or box of shittim wood, without a lid or a bottom, five cubits
long, five wide and three high. Inside and outside, it was covered with
thick plates of bronze. Along the top of the four sides there was a
flat, projecting ridge, the "surround", and protruding from that ridge,
on the four corners, were the horns. Under the surround there was a
kind of grating with rings attached to it, through which the staves
could be passed. "In my opinion," Mr. Schouten writes, "the cavity
or inside of the altar was filled with earth (to accord with Exodus
20: 24). According to Exodus 40: 6, the altar was to be placed "before
the door of the tabernacle", whereas the laver was to be set between
the tent of the congregation and the altar, so that on entering, one
would first see the altar of the burnt offering (B), and then the laver
(C). This has been interpreted as symbolic of firstly Christ's justification
and then His sanctification. Nothing is said in the Bible about the
shape or form of the laver, only that Bezaleel "made the laver of
brass and the foot of it of brass" (Exod. 38: 8). The tabernacle (D)
stood fifty cubits from the east side. The tent consisted of forty-eight
boards of shittim wood, covered by four kinds of curtains. The first
curtains were made of fine twined linen and the basic colour was white,
but sky blue, purple and scarlet were woven into it "with cunning
work". The second set of curtains were of goat's hair, and over them
were hung curtains of rams' skins dyed scarlet. The fourth or outer
cover was, according to the A.V., made of badgers' skins; they were
probably the skins of seals or dugongs. These were fixed on three
sides by means of cords and bronze pins driven into the ground on these
same sides, to which the cords were fastened and securely tightened.
The tent was divided into two parts: the Holy Place and the Holy of
Holies.

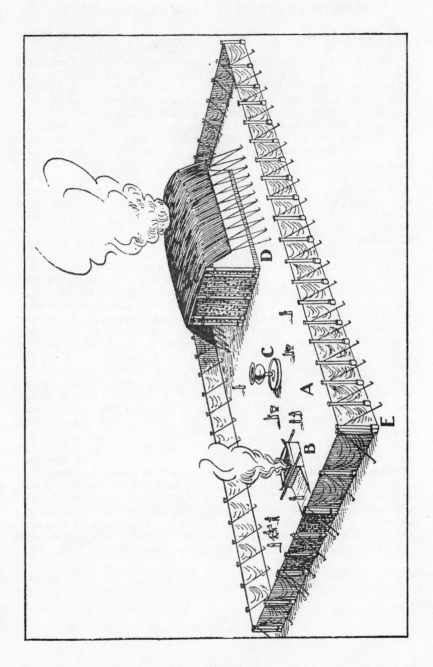

48. HIGH PRIEST ON THE DAY OF ATONEMENT

The High Priest on the Day of Atonement in the Holy of Holies (the Rev. L. Schouten Hzn). The Holy of Holies was the place for (e) the Ark of the Covenant (Num. 10: 33), or Ark of the Testimony (Exod. 25: 22), the Ark of the Lord, the Lord of all the earth (Joshua 3: 13), the Ark of the Covenant of the Lord of hosts, which dwelleth between the cherubims (1 Sam. 4: 4), the ark of God's strength (Ps. 132: 8). The Ark was made of shittim wood (Exod. 25: 10), and was two and a half cubits long and one and a half cubits wide and high. The Ark was covered inside and out with pure gold, and on the top of the Ark was the mercy seat (Exod. 25: 21), round which there was a gold moulding (f). At the four corners there were four gold rings which held two shittim wood bars covered with gold. Two cherubs (g) stood on the mercy seat with their wings extended, facing inwards and looking downwards. Between the cherubims and above them could sometimes be seen the *Shekinah* (h), the visible sign of God's presence among Israel above the wings of the cherubims of the Ark of the Covenant, the literal fulfilment by means of this sign of what God had promised when He commanded that the tabernacle should be built: "Let them make me a sanctuary, that I may dwell among them" (Exod. 25: 8). The High Priest entered the Holy of Holies on the Day of Atonement on the tenth day of the month *Tishri* (Lev. 16: 1–34; Lev. 23: 26–32; Num. 29: 7–11); and on this occasion he wore special robes (Exod. 39: 41): the holy linen tunic (a), the linen girdle and the linen mitre (b) (Lev. 16: 4). His clothes were of white linen, since white was symbolic of his act of atonement (Heb. 9: 24; 7: 26). The first occasion on which the High Priest entered is described in Leviticus 16: 12, 13: "And he shall take a censer full of burning coals of fire from off the altar before the Lord, and his hands full of sweet incense beaten small, and bring it within the veil". So while the Holy of Holies was filling with clouds of sweet incense, the High Priest went outside and took from the priest in the court the golden patera (c) containing the blood of the bullock of the sin-offering, in order to re-enter the Holy of Holies and make atonement for himself and his house. He dipped the first finger of his right hand in the blood of the steer and sprinkled it in the centre of the mercy seat, between the cherubims. Then he dipped his finger again into the blood of the sin-offering and this time sprinkled the floor in front of the mercy seat and the Ark, and repeated this seven times. Having returned once again to the court, one of the goats was slain as a sacrifice of the people, and for the third time he entered the Holy of Holies and sprinkled the blood in the same way, this time as an atonement for the people.

49. THE HOLY PLACE

1. The Holy Place was separated from the Holy of Holies by the veil (F) hanging from four pillars. The walls on the right and left consisted of wooden boards. On the south side (Exod. 40: 24) stood the candlestick (A) or rather, candelabrum (Exod. 25: 6; 35: 8), for light in the sanctuary was provided by "pure oil of olives beaten for the light" (Exod. 27: 20). It was a work of art of pure gold. Three pairs of branches sprang from the shaft rising straight from the base, and the shaft and six branches all terminated at the same height. At each of these seven points were "bowls like unto almonds" to hold the lamps of oil. Beneath these bowls were decorations of knobs and flowers (Exod. 25: 35). The lights of the lamps in the almonds on the branches burn "over against it" (Exod. 25: 37, which Moffatt renders as "so that they shine in front of it"). There were a number of small implements belonging to the candlestick, "tongs" and "snuff-dishes" (D on the left). Immediately opposite the candlestick, on the north side (Exod. 40: 22) was the table of the Shewbread (C), a description of which can be found in Exodus 25: 23–30; 37: 10–16. The table was made of shittim wood overlaid with pure gold. The top was surrounded by a frame of a hand's breadth with mouldings in gold above and below it (C). The table stood on four legs, each having a gold ring through which the bars (H) were passed. A number of vessels were used at the table: dishes, bowls or pans (presumably smaller bowls for frankincense, "that it may be on the bread for a memorial", Lev. 24: 7, 8); pots (or squat jars) and jars (sacrificial beakers). The bread consisted of twelve cakes in two rows, six in each row (G), "upon the pure table before the Lord" (Lev. 24: 6, "and . . . pure frankincense upon each row", 24: 7). The Altar of Incense (B) (Exod. 30: 1–7; 37: 25–8), was made of shittim wood overlaid with pure gold, and had four horns at the corners. In Exodus 30: 7, 8 it is said of Aaron that he would burn incense upon it. Aaron used it at the consecration of the Tabernacle, at his entering upon the priesthood and, as did also the High Priests after him, on the Day of Atonement, on the Sabbath, on the Feast of the New Moon and at certain other great feasts. (It is one such feast that is illustrated here, where the High Priest stands near the Altar of Incense.) The incense consisted of four ingredients (Exod. 30: 34–6), and it is from this perfume that David draws his analogy, "Let my prayer be set forth before thee as incense" (Ps. 141: 2).

2. The Molten Sea (made of bronze). The height of the bronze laver (*a*) is about eight feet, the diameter of the top is about 16 feet, and its thickness is a hand's breadth. The laver stood on four teams of three oxen (*b*), all made of bronze (1 Kings 7: 23ff; 2 Chron. 4: 2ff).

3. Two possible reconstructions of the pillars Jachin and Boaz. The capitals are enclosed in a tracery of bronze with two rows of pomegranates.

The court of the Temple (reproduction from Ch. Chipiez and G. Perrot). At the back of the court in the porch of the Temple, were the pillars Jachin and Boaz (*b* and *c*). The height of these enormous bronze pillars (1 Kings 7: 15ff); 2 Kings 25: 13ff; 2 Chron. 3: 15ff; Jer. 52: 21ff) was eighteen cubits (30 feet), "and a line of twelve cubits did compass either of them about" (1 Kings 7: 15), which gives a diameter of 3·90 cubits (i.e. six feet), "the thickness thereof was four fingers: it was hollow" (Jer. 52: 21). On the top of the column was a capital of five cubits (eight feet high), enclosed in a bronze tracery with two rows of pomegranates, a hundred in each. What exactly these capitals looked like we do not know (see plate 49, 3). Presumably they stood in front of the Temple and were not used as supports. In between the pillars (at *h*) is the doorway into the entrance hall, having a double door of cypress wood; the doorposts were made of olive wood. The wall round it was built of massive stone blocks "stone made ready before it was brought thither: so that there was neither hammer nor axe nor any tool of iron heard in the house, while it was in building" (1 Kings 6: 7). The Temple of Solomon stood in a large court (*a*). It is assumed that the floor was paved with stone slabs. This courtyard is called in the Bible "the inner court" (1 Kings 6: 37; 7: 12). Before the Exile, people had free access to this inner court where the crowd gathered at the festivals (Isa. 1: 12). In this inner court was the large Altar of Burnt Offering (*d, e*), the Molten Sea (only just visible at *i*) and the movable lavers of brass (*f*). The Altar of Burnt Offering was a stately edifice of stone. To the east of the altar, according to the description in Ezekiel 43: 17, was a flight of steps (in the Temple of Herod the approach was on the south side, and there were no steps, in accordance with the ancient decree in Exodus 20: 26). To the right and left of this Altar of Burnt Offering were five movable lavers (*f*). These were pots of bronze, holding about 320 gallons, placed on stands with a square base having sides of six feet, and nearly five feet high, made of a framework of strips of bronze (Professor J. de Groot). These lavers (as they are called in 1 Kings 7: 38) held 40 bath (and 1 bath = 6 hin = 36·44 litres, so that 40 bath is 40 x 36·44 litres = 1,457·6 litres or 323·9 gallons). Nowadays, however, it is generally assumed that the bath is equal to 4·85 gallons. The framework of the stands was decorated with lions, oxen and cherubs (1 Kings 7: 29), and the lavers moved on wheels (1 Kings 7: 33).

The inner court may have been surrounded by a colonnade (according to Chipiez's and Perrot's reconstruction), and the temple buildings were surrounded by annexes (*g*).

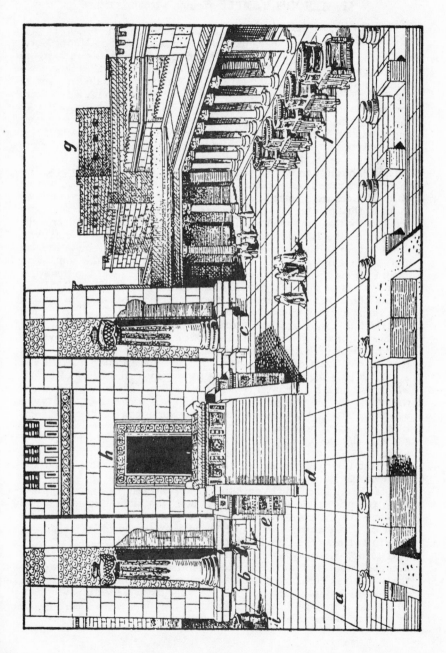

51. HEROD'S TEMPLE (Schick's reconstruction)

The bridge in the foreground spans the brook Cedron (2 Sam. 15: 23; John 18: 1). The vast, spacious enclosure was situated on Mount Moria (2 Chron. 3: 1) or Mount Zion (1 Macc. 14: 26). To the east of the Temple court stretches the dazzling white colonnade (c) called Solomon's Porch (John 10: 23; Acts 3: 11; 5: 12). The most magnificent part of the Temple is the Royal Porch of Herod (b) on the south side, where the twelve-year-old Jesus sat among the doctors (Luke 2: 46). At the north-west corner is the ancient citadel Baris, rebuilt, strengthened and renamed Antonia (k) by Herod the Great. The A.V. calls this a castle (Acts 21: 34) and Moffatt a barracks. Steps (j) lead up from the Temple court to the citadel (Paul standing on the stairs, Acts 21: 40). The large court (p) on the south side is the Court of the Gentiles; there was a raised terrace, surrounded by a low wall (d), in the middle of it. Notices were posted on pillars forbidding all who were not Jews to pass this point. It was therefore a serious accusation that was· brought by the Jews of Asia Minor against Paul that he had brought Greeks into the Temple and had polluted the Holy Place (Acts 21: 28). Steps led up to the terrace which gave access to the Temple by any one of nine gateways, four on the north side, four on the south and one on the east; this last was the main gate (at e) called "the Beautiful Gate" (Acts 3: 2), which led to the Court of the Women (f). There during the Feast of Tabernacles two large candlesticks were placed, and every evening the crowds would assemble with burning torches and the lights were lit midst great rejoicing. There may be a reference to this in Christ's words, "I am the light of the world; who follows me shall not walk in darkness but shall have the light of life" (John 8: 12). Here in the Court of the Women was also "the treasury" (Mark 12: 41–4). A long flight of fifteen steps (i) led up to the Court of Israel, which was on a higher level (g). It may well have been on these steps that Anna the prophetess praised the Lord and where the aged Simeon was filled with joy because he had seen "the light to lighten the Gentiles" (who were walking outside in the Temple court) and "to be the glory of thy people Israel", who were allowed to approach the Holy Place (Luke 2: 25–38). The inner Court of Israel was separated from the inner Court of the Priests (h) by a low parapet; here stood the Altar of the Burnt Offering and the lavers. Twelve steps on the west side of the Altar led to the entrance hall of the Temple, and from these steps the priests blessed the people; here too, dumbstruck Zacharias beckoned to the people (Luke 1: 22). Beyond the entrance hall were the Holy Place and the Holy of Holies, separated by the veil that was rent in twain at the Crucifixion (Matt. 27: 51).

It is not known with any certainty where "the pinnacles of the Temple" were, but they are often identified with the high tower at the south-east corner, overlooking the Cedron valley (at m). To the west of the Temple there used to be a valley, the valley of Tyropœon which has since been filled in; a bridge (n) led across the valley to the upper city of Jerusalem.

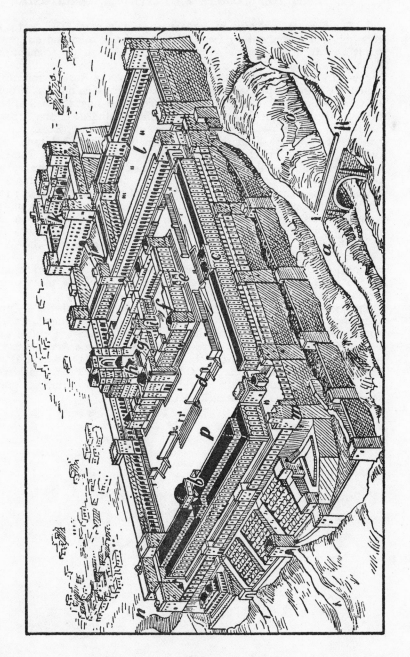

52. TEMPLE ENCLOSURE AND CITADEL OF ANTONIA

1. The Temple enclosure in Jerusalem as it is now. The centre of this holy place is about 13 feet higher and forms a second enclosure (as it used to in the original Temple court; Jeremiah 36: 10 mentions "the higher court"). Wide steps lead from the lower part to the higher. In the middle rises the famous Dome of the Rock (erroneously called the Mosque of Omar since it is neither a mosque nor was it built by Omar). Smaller buildings have been erected against the wall of this terrace; they are schools and dwellings that remind us of the "chambers of the priests" who kept "the charge of the house" (Ezek. 40: 17, 38, 45; 46: 19). Each chamber was called after the inhabitant, who might receive visitors there (cf. Ezra 10: 6). The magnificent Dome of the Rock dominates the enclosure. According to tradition, the marble used was part of the treasures set aside by David for the Temple (1 Chron. 29: 2). Inside is the famous "rock of the plain" (Jer. 21: 13), on which at one time stood the Altar of the Burnt Offering in the Temple Court. In the background is the Mount of Olives, on the northern spur of which, Mount Scopus, is the Hebrew University. To the right of the Dome, on the Mount of Olives, can be seen the "Viri Galilei", Men of Galilee (Acts 1: 11).

Down in the valley, near the dark olive grove, is Gethsemane, and to the right of that Dominus Flevit, assumed to be the place where Jesus wept (Luke 19: 41–4).

2. Reconstruction of Antonia. To the north west of the Temple there was a strong citadel in the times of the New Testament. It was the ancient tower of Baris, rebuilt by Herod the Great, fortified and renamed Antonia. This citadel is called a castle in the A.V. (Acts 21: 34). A flight of steps led from the Temple Court to the citadel (Paul standing on the stairs, Acts 21: 40). This citadel is often considered to have been the court-house in which Pilate resided during the great feasts. Moffatt calls it a barracks (Acts 21: 35).

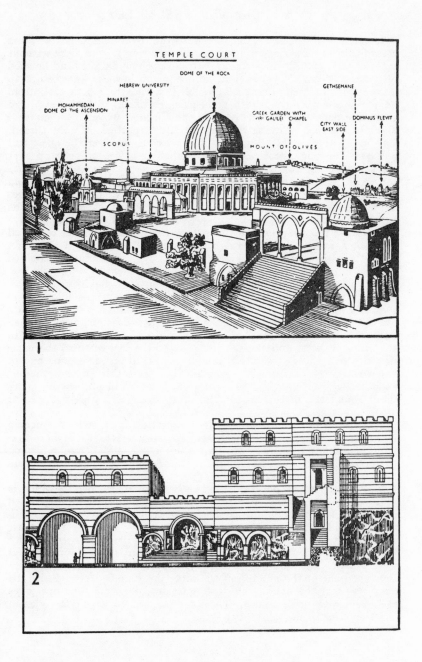

TEMPLE COURT

1

2

53. HOLY MEN, PHYLACTERY

1. High Priest. The High Priest wore over his priestly robes the robe of the Ephod, an upper garment woven in one piece without seam or join, of a sky-blue colour, with an opening for the head finished off with a collar, sleeveless, and falling just below the knees so as to leave the white linen priest's coat visible underneath. Round its bottom hem it was embellished with pomegranates made of double-stranded yarn alternating with bells of gold; the Ephod woven in a mixture of violet, purple, carmine and white with a pattern in gold thread. This garment probably consisted of two parts, one over the chest and one over the back, fastened by two shoulder pieces brought up over the shoulders and fixed at the front; the whole was tied tightly round the waist. On the shoulders were fastened two onyx stones set in gold rosettes, and engraved on them were the names of the twelve tribes of Israel, six on each stone. A breastplate was hung on top of the Ephod, and this was folded double to form a kind of pouch. Twelve jewels were mounted on the front, four rows of three each, engraved with the names of the twelve tribes of Israel. The Urim and Thummin were placed in the pouch for safe keeping. A mitre or turban covered the head, and by means of a violet band a diadem of pure gold was attached to it, bearing the inscription "Holiness to the Lord".

2 and 3. Priests (cf. Professor J. de Groot). The priests officiating in the Holy Place wore these vestments: a long tunic with sleeves of white linen, woven throughout without a seam, white drawers, a white linen mitre wound like a turban, but cone-shaped, and a girdle woven in the same material and the same colours as the veil of the Tabernacle (Exod. 39: 29). "Both ends of the girdle draped on the ground except when the priest was officiating, when they were thrown over the left shoulder (2). This girdle was several yards long and was wound many times round the body between the armpits and the hips" (Professor J. de Groot).

4. A Nazarite. The figure in the illustration is in fact no longer a Nazarite. On laying aside his vows, the Nazarite took the hair that had been shorn from his head in his left hand, and before returning to normal life, he would have to make the offerings ordained in Numbers 6: 13ff.

5. Phylacteries (*te phillin*). These are strips of leather to which is attached a very strong, square box made of parchment and painted black (*a*). The box contains four parts of the Thora written on parchment: Exodus 13: 1 and 11: 6; Deuteronomy 6: 4–9; 11: 13–21. According to Deuteronomy 6: 4–9 two phylacteries were used, one for the head and one for the arm. These (called frontlets in Deuteronomy) were put on in such a way that one box rested on the head, between the eyes (seat of the mind) and the other on the left arm opposite the heart (seat of the actions and the emotions, denoting that one loves the Lord with one's heart). They are referred to as phylacteries in the New Testament (Matt. 23: 5).

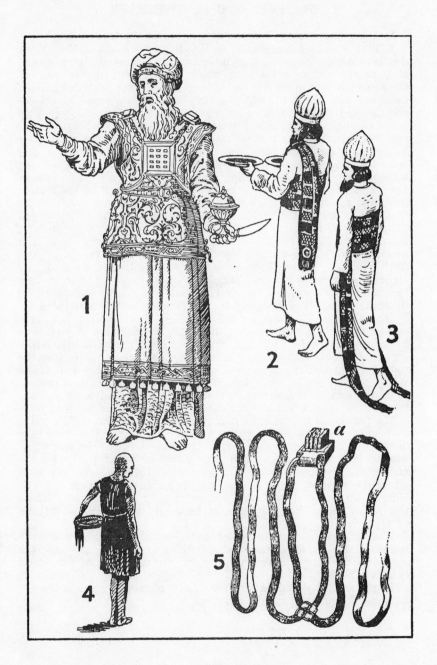

54. SYNAGOGUE AT CAPERNAUM

1. **The synagogue at Capernaum** as it was in the first century.

2. **View inside the synagogue** (see Heinrich Kohl and Carl Watzinger, *Antike Synagogen in Galilee*). The old ruins of the ancient synagogue at Capernaum stand on a promontory jutting out into the sea, and the lower part of the walls is still standing. Until 1905 it was a derelict ruin, but between that year and 1921 explorations were carried out and detailed investigations were made. Franciscan monks who were put in charge of the site have attempted to piece the available fragments together in such a way that we now have some idea of the appearance of the synagogue. And the archaeologists Kohl and Watzinger in their book on ancient synagogues in Galilee have published drawings giving a reconstruction of this building at Capernaum. This might well be the synagogue of which the gospel says that it was built by the Roman centurion for the Jews (Luke 7: 5). The archaeologist Orfali insists that this is indeed the building in which Jesus taught (John 6: 59). Other experts, however, are of the opinion that the synagogue dates from the end of the second century (between 190 and 225 A.D.), "but there is complete agreement that Jesus undoubtedly taught on this site" (Obbink). It was built on a terrace 10 feet wide, on a slightly higher level than the shore. The doors of the building were reached by climbing four steps at the western (left) end of this terrace, or by thirteen steps to the east (right), a difference that is accounted for by the slope of the land towards the east. The building ran north and south, with the front facing the south, the direction of Jerusalem towards which the Jews turned for prayers. From the terrace the building could be entered by one of three doors; the fourth doorway on the right led to a courtyard enclosed on the west side by the wall of the synagogue and on the other three sides by colonnades. The synagogues in Galilee had three doors at the front. The courtyard probably contained a fountain where people could wash their hands and feet.

The interior of the building had colonnades along three of its walls, over which were (probably) places for the women (*f*). The stone floor in the centre (still preserved) is then the ancient site of the synagogue where Christ must have walked; this would be where He healed the man with the withered hand (Luke 6: 6), and where He taught, and where He cured the man possessed of an unclean spirit (Mark 1: 21–8). Here Christ spoke of the bread that came down from heaven—"these things said he in the synagogue, as he taught in Capernaum" (John 6: 59).

Just inside the door was a rostrum on which was a desk where the scrolls of the law were read, and the chest or ark (*c*) containing the scrolls of the prophets and holy books. On each side of this stood candlesticks.

To the left (at *g*) can be seen the courtyard, above which is the undulating sky-line of the hilly country.

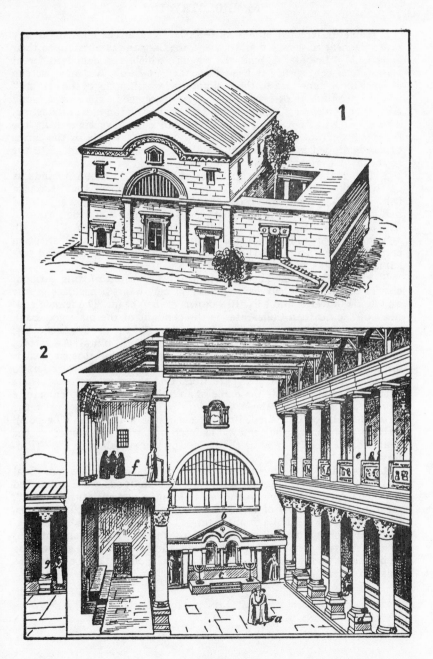

55. IDOLATRY (1)

1. Maṣṣēbās (erected stones at Gezer). "Inside the city, or at any rate very near to it, was a place where the Canaanites worshipped their gods (A.V. "heights"). Such a "height" which was honoured for at least fifteen centuries, has been unearthed at Gezer, and now we can at least form some idea of the well known "worshipping of the heights" which the prophets of Israel for so long denounced. Here were found a number of *menhirs*, among which the smallest is the most interesting. The upper half of it has a polish that can only have come from the repeated touch of devout lips kissing the stone fervently or the caress of hands dipped in blood or oil, anointing the stone in homage to the godhead" (A. Noordtzij). Cf 1 Kings 19: 18.

2. Babylonian godhead in the form of a fish. "This god reminds us of the Philistine god Dagon. It is generally assumed that it was a fish-god. It appears from 1 Samuel 5 that the image of Dagon at Ashdod had a head and arms. As to whether his lower half took the form of a fish depends on whether the reading "the fishy part" (A.V. margin 1 Sam. 5: 4) should be substituted for "stump". If this substitution is made, then Dagon had the head and upper body of a man and presumably a fish's tail" (A. Noordtzij).

3. Female Godhead. The figure is wrapped in a tight-fitting garment clearly revealing the curves of the body. She wears a necklace, girdle and ankle bracelet, and a Hittite crown on her head. The female godhead of the heathen Canaanites is the pendant of the male god Baal, with whom she is frequently associated (Judges 2: 13; 10: 6; 1 Sam. 7: 4; 12: 10). Her name is Astarte, in Hebrew Ashtoreth, plural: Ashtaroth, alternatively Asherah. The A.V. talks of "groves", but it is clear that, for instance, "the prophets of the groves" (1 Kings 18: 19) refers to servants of this goddess. (Apart from this the word *asherah* occurs with another meaning as the name of an object belonging to Canaanite worship; it is true that the A.V. had "groves" for this too, but at the most this object is a single tree or even just a tree trunk or pole). Astarte represented the female life force and was worshipped as the source of all fertility, and as the generator and sustainer of life" (Professor G. C. Aalders).

4. Baal. The name given to the heathen Canaanites' male god. Baal was originally not a proper name; because the gods were not called by their names, this one was given the vague nomenclature "ba'al", meaning lord or owner of certain holy wells, trees, animals, mountains, stones or places. The Canaanites prayed to these local *Ba'als* for fertility for their soil and all good gifts (Hosea 2: 4). The worship of Baal in the days of Ahab and Jezebel was addressed to the god of the Phoenicians, so that it was a national and religious obligation to oppose this practice.

1. Moloch (according to St. Vincent). The word "Moloch" really means the same as "melek", meaning king. Moloch was presumably just another name for Baal as a destructive force, or he was one of the numerous *Ba'als* of Canaan. In Jeremiah 32: 35 Moloch and Baal are considered as one and the same. Moloch is the god of the consuming sun who was worshipped in the rite of "passing through the fire" (Lev. 18: 21; 2 Kings 23: 10). Moloch as shown here is a bull's head, reminiscent also of the worship of calves (1 Kings 12: 28), and expresses the idea of sensual worship by means of the male organ carved in the forehead above the nose. The authenticity of this image is, however, disputed.

2. Babylonian replica of the liver. Soothsaying with the aid of a liver (hepatoscopy) figured prominently in Babylonian life. No two sheep's livers are quite alike. Taking advantage of this fact, they devised a complete system of predicting the future from the appearance of the liver of sacrificial animals. Hence in Ezekiel's vision in Ezekiel 21: 21, "the king of Babylon stood at the parting of the way, at the head of the two ways, to use divination: he made his arrows bright, he consulted with images, he looked in the liver". The liver was also considered to be the source of life and the centre of the emotions in Israel (Prov. 7: 23; Lam. 2: 11). But the law of Israel made these superstitious practices impossible by ordaining that the "caul that is above the liver" of the sacrificial animals should be burned (Exod. 29: 13; Lev. 3: 4, 5: 4: 9–11).

3. "Assyrian" gods. Relief of Tiglath-Pileser at Calah. Assyrian soldiers with pointed battle helmets are carrying idols, perhaps as loot, in which case they cannot be Assyrian gods. The two in the front (*a, b*) appear to be female gods; both are seated. The third god is almost entirely hidden in a case (*c*). The fourth (*d*) is a god of lightning, with fork lightning in the left hand and an axe in the right. The procession could, however, be a parade of Assyrian might, superior to the power of the gods of the people (Isa. 26: 19; 2 Kings 18: 34).

Such was the way the gods were transported by men. This is therefore in striking contrast with the God of Israel, who carries and delivers his people. In the words of Isaiah: "Bel boweth down, Nebo stoopeth, their idols were upon the beasts, and upon the cattle" (Isa. 46: 1), and he goes on to bear witness to God's promise, "even to hoar hairs will I carry you" (Isa. 46: 4). Hence the disdain with which he speaks of the heathen who carry their graven images (45: 20).

4. Image of the goddess Diana in the temple at Ephesus. Diana, the Latin name for the Greek goddess Artemis, was held in great honour in Greece and the Middle East. The worship of Artemis of Ephesus, "Diana of the Ephesians" had spread far and wide ("whom all Asia and the world worshippeth", Acts 19: 27). Originally the worship of this goddess was an oriental form of worshipping nature, so that the image of Diana was given various symbolic features expressing fertility and vitality. Reproductions of Diana were placed as votive offerings in the homes of those who worshipped her (Acts 19: 24).

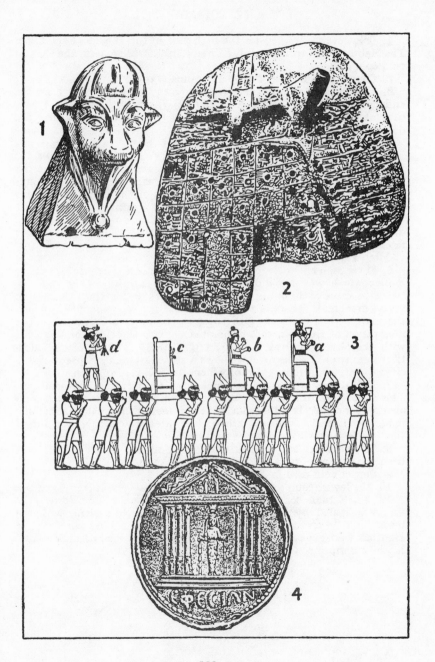

57. COINAGE

1. **Coins** are mentioned for the first time in the Bible in Ezra 2: 69. The Hebrew word translated by "drams" is "*dărkĕmŏnim*", the Persian gold coin *daric*.

2. **Coin from the time of John Hyrcanus** (135–106).

3. **Half shekel,** A.D.4. The obverse shows two bundles of branches and between them a citron (the *'ethrŏgh* which, with the *lŭlābh*, was used at the Feast of Tabernacles). The reverse bears the legend "the deliverance of Zion".

4. **Coin dating from the time of Herod the Great.**

5. **Silver denarius,** called penny in the A.V. (Matt. 20: 2; Luke 10: 35; John 12: 5). According to Matthew 22: 19, the denarius was the tribute required of every Israelite by the Roman ruler, and was therefore called tribute money. The head is that of the emperor Tiberius (Luke 3: 1) and the legend reads in Latin: TI (berius) CAESAR DIVI AUG(usti) F(ilius) AUGUSTUS, (i.e. "Tiberius, emperor, son of the divine Augustus, the illustrious, cf. Mark 12: 16). The legend on the reverse is a continuation of the imperial title: PONTIF(ex) MAXIM(us) .. High Priest.

6. **Silver stater.** In Matthew 17: 24–7 there is a reference to tribute money which was one didrachma (see A.V. margin). This coin had twice the value of the one mentioned in Luke 15: 8 (for which the margin gives: drachma). There is also mention of "a piece of money", which the margin calls a stater, with twice the value of a didrachma. The illustration of this coin shows the obverse with the effigy of Augustus with the Greek inscription KAISAROS SEBASTOU ("of the illustrious emperor"). The reverse shows a seated woman representing the city of Antioch, a monogram of which, ANTX, is also given.

7. In Matthew 10: 29 mention is made of "one farthing" (an *assarion*). This *assarion* or *as* was a copper coin worth four *quàdrans*, which were also copper coins. It is this coin, the *quadrans*, which is called a farthing in Mark 12: 42. The widow "threw in two mites, which make a farthing" (i.e. two *leptons* with a value of one *quadrans*).

8. **The smallest copper coin of Herod Antipas,** which might have been the widow's "mite" (Mark 12: 42; Luke 21: 1–4).

9. **Copper coin used in Nero's reign.**

10, 11. **Jewish coins** minted during Bar Kokhba's revolt (132–135 A.D.).

12, 13. **Roman coins** recording the subjugation of the Jews. The first was issued by Vespasian after the fall of Jerusalem, with the inscription "Judaea capta"; the second was issued by the emperor Hadrian who gave occupied Jerusalem the name that is abbreviated in the inscription, COL(onia) AEL(ia) CAP(itolina).

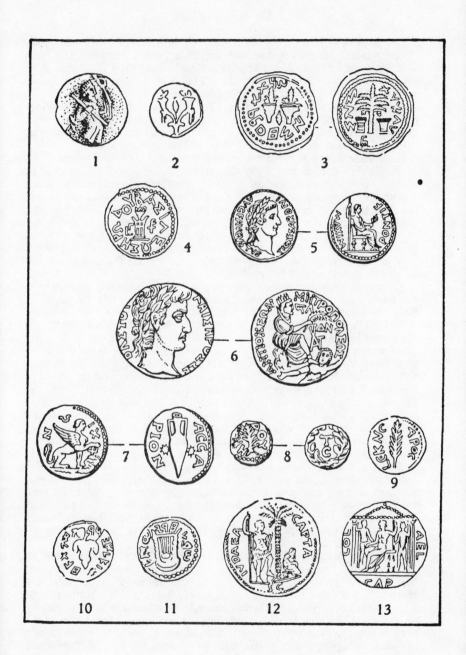

58. MATRIMONY

1. "Spread therefore thy skirt over thine handmaid" (Ruth 3: 9). "Now when I passed by thee, and looked upon thee, behold, thy time was the time of love; and I spread my skirt over thee . . . and thou becamest mine" (Ezek. 16: 8). In token that a man took his future wife unto him, he spread the tip of his upper garment over her.

2. **The bridegroom and his train.** The custom of escorting the bridegroom in procession to his bride survives to the present day. Towards midnight, as the bridegroom approaches the bride's home, the warning cry goes up "Go ye out to meet him" (Matt. 25: 1–6).

3. **A bride adorned for her husband** (Rev. 21: 2). It was the duty of the bride's friends and female members of the household to get her ready so that she would appear at her best before the bridegroom. Even in the days of ancient Israel, the bride with all her adornments was referred to as the symbol of festive joy, whether secular or spiritual. In Isaiah 61: 10 the prophet says: "I will greatly rejoice in the Lord, my soul shall be joyful in my God; for he hath clothed me with the garments of salvation, he hath covered me with the robe of righteousness, as the bridegroom decketh himself with ornaments, and as a bride adorneth herself with her jewels".

When the bridegroom has come in, he may lift up the veil and see the bride's face. At that moment he says, nowadays: "In the name of God, the Merciful and Gracious", and he greets her with "The evening is blessed", to which she meekly replied "May God bless you". To show that he takes pleasure in his bride he utters a joyful cry of surprise. The women and the bridegroom's friends stand outside, eagerly waiting to take up the cry and echo his joy. It was to this that John the Baptist referred when he said: "He that hath the bride is the bridegroom: but the friend of the bridegroom, which standeth and heareth him, rejoiceth greatly because of the bridegroom's voice: this my joy therefore is fulfilled" (John 3: 29). John rejoiced that Christ, the true bridegroom, delighted in the Bride whom John had prepared for His coming.

It is, then, of the utmost importance that the bridegroom should not be disappointed at the first glimpse of his wife. Everything possible is done to enhance her grace and beauty, "Though thou rentest thy face with painting, in vain shalt thou make thyself fair" (Jer. 4: 30). In Ezra 23: 40 the prophet reproaches the women: "ye have sent for men to come from far, for whom thou didst wash thyself, paintedst thy eyes and deckedst thyself with ornaments". And Jeremiah asks the question "Can a maid forget her ornaments, or a bride her attire?" (Jer. 2: 32, Moffatt).

4. **Bill of Divorcement.** Seven times the Bible mentions a bill of divorcement: Deuteronomy 24: 1, 3; Isaiah 50: 1; Jeremiah 3: 8; Matthew 5: 31; 19: 7; Mark 10: 4. It was intended as a deterrent rather than a legalization (Deut. 24: 2–4; Matt. 19: 8; Mark 10: 5). The Jewish lawyers busied themselves with all sorts of problems relating to the bill of divorcement: what kind of writing material should be used when drawing it up, how it should be worded, whether or not it would be legally binding, etc. This was the reason for their insistence on certain standard formulae.

59. STREET SCENES

1. A child carried on the shoulder. In speaking of the great services which the Jews would receive at the hands of the heathen peoples who had oppressed them, when they were restored to their own land, God promises in the words of the prophet Isaiah (49: 22): "I will lift up mine hand to the Gentiles, and set up my standard to the people: and they shall bring thy sons in their arms, and thy daughters shall be carried upon their shoulders". Eastern women carry their children on their shoulders right from babyhood.

2. Prosperous Jew from Menecha in Arabia. On his shoulder he has the key to his business premises which are in the bazaar quarter. Carrying keys on the shoulder is a very ancient custom: "and the key of the house of David will I lay upon his shoulder; so he shall open and none shall shut; and he shall shut, and none shall open" (Isa. 22: 22). .The keys then in use were made of wood and were of a considerable size. Eliakim carried the wooden key on his shoulder, and to him alone was granted the power to open and close the doors of the palace. So Eliakim is a prototype of Christ (Rev. 3: 7) and of the ministers in the New Testament (Matt. 16: 19).

3. The farmer's wife carrying to the town fuel in the form of dried, flat cakes of dung and straw. The woman has stacked the dung, on top of which are two leather bundles, on a flat board of matted straw. The dung and straw slabs are used for fuel.

4. Porter. The weight that these men can lift is often astounding. These porters (*hamals*) are a common sight in towns since the streets are too narrow for carts, so that they are in frequent demand. The porter and his burden are often used metaphorically in the Bible. Moses complains "that thou layest the burden of all this people upon me", alluding here to the crushing weight of the responsibility of having to lead the ungrateful Israelites through the desert until he was relieved of his burden by the election of the seventy elders (Num. 11: 11–25). David cries out in his anguish: "mine iniquities are gone over mine head: as an heavy burden they are too heavy for me" (Ps. 38: 4). Christ makes use of the same metaphor in speaking of the ceremonies imposed by the scribes and Pharisees on the people, reproaching them in the words "For they bind heavy burdens and grievous to be borne, and lay them on men's shoulders; but they themselves will not move them with one of their fingers" (Matt. 23: 4). In contrast to this He says of Himself, "my burden is light" (Matt. 11: 30).

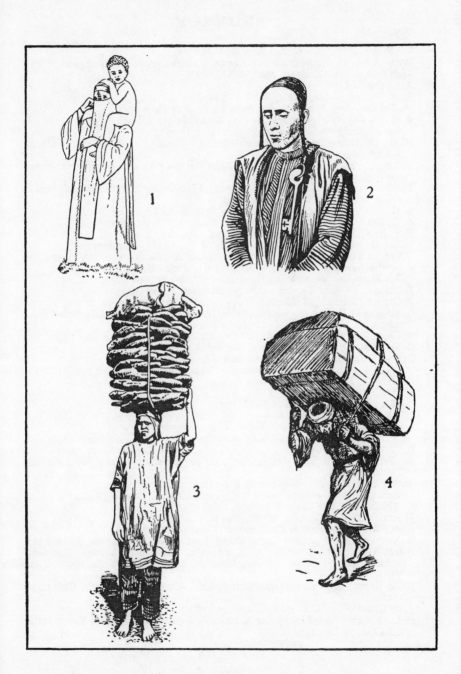

BIBLIOGRAPHY

W. F. Albright. The Archaeology of Palestine.
W. F. Albright. From the Stone Age to Christianity, Baltimore 1946.
Archäologischer Anzeiger. 1907; XXII.
Ars Antiqua III.
A. E. Bailey. Daily Life in Bible Times, New York 1943.
H. Balmer. Die Romfahrt des Apostels Paulus, Bern 1905.
A. G. Barrois, O.P. Manuel d'Archéologie Biblique I, Paris 1939.
I. Benzinger. Hebräische Archäologie, Leipzig 1927.
F. M. Th. Böhl. De geschiedenis der stad Sichem en de opgravingen aldaar, Amsterdam 1926.
F. M. Th. Böhl. Palestina in het licht der jongste opgravingen en onderzoekingen, Amsterdam 1931.
Tj. Bottema en Prof. Dr. Joh. de Groot. Platen voor het Bijbels onderwijs in school en catechisatie, Wageningen.
A. C. Bouquet. Everyday Life in New Testament Times, Batsford.
A. C. Bouquet. Everyday Life in Old Testament Times, Batsford.
F. J. Bruijel. Bijbel en Natuur, Kampen 1939.
Millar Burrows. The Dead Sea Scrolls of S. Mark's Monastery.
Vol. I. The Isaiah Manuscript and the Habakkuk Commentary. Published by the American Schools of Oriental Research. New Haven 1950.
Millar Burrows. What Mean these Stones? New Haven 1941.
J. Capart. Thèbes. La gloire d'un grand passé, Bruxelles 1925.
J. Capart. Memphis à l'ombre des pyramides, Bruxelles 1930.
C. Chipiez et G. Perrot. Le temple de Jérusalem et la maison du bois Liban, restitués d'après Ezéchiel et le Livre des Rois, Paris 1889.
V. Christian. Altertumskunde des Zweistromlandes, I, II, Leipzig 1940.
G. Dalman. Orte und Wege Jesu, Gütersloh 1921.
Gustaf Dalman. Arbeit und Sitte in Palästina, Gütersloh.
  I. 1. Jahreslauf und Tageslauf. Herbst und Winter 1928.
      2. Frühling und Sommer 1928.
  II. Der Ackerbau, 1932.
  III. Von der Ernte zum Mehl, 1933.
  IV. Brot, Oel, Wein, 1935.
  V.   Webstoff, Spinnen, Weben, Kleidung, 1937.
  VI. Zeltleben, Vieh und Milchwirtschaft, Jagd und Fischfang, 1939.
R. Dussaud. Le prophète Jérémie et les lettres de Lakish, Syria 1938.
A. Erman, H. Ranke. Aegypten und aegyptisches Leben im Altertum, Tübingen 1923.
Jack Finegan. Light from the Ancient Past, Princeton 1947.
L. Fonck, S.J. Streifzüge durch die biblische Flora, Freiburg 1900.
H. Forczyner. The Lachish Letters, 1938.
J. Friedrich. Ras Sjamra, Leipzig 1933.
Kurt Galling. Biblisches Reallexikon, Tübingen 1937.
H. Gressmann. Altorientalische Bilder zum Alten Testament, Berlin 1927.
Hilma Granquist. Marriage Customs in a Palestinian Village. (Societas Scientiarum Fennica. Commentationes humaniorum litterarum. Tom. VI; 1935.)
J. de Groot. De Palestijnsche achtergrond van den Pentateuch, Gröningen 1928.
J. de Groot. I en II Samuël. Tekst en Uitleg. Gröningen 1934, 1935.
P. L. O. Guy. New Light from Armageddon (Oriental Institute Communications No. 9), Chicago.

BIBLIOGRAPHY

A. Th. Hartman. Die Hebräerin am Putztische und als Braut, Amsterdam.
F. G. Hayne. Getreue Dastellung und Beschreibung der in der Arzneykunde
  gebräuchlichen Gewächse, VII, VIII, IX, X, Berlin 1821–1825.
C. Hülsen. Form und Palatin, München.
A. Jeremias. Das Alte Testament im Lichte des Alten Orients, Leipzig 1916.
R. Kittel. Het Oude Testament in het licht der nieuwe onderzoekingen.
  Bewerkt door Dr. H. W. Obbink. Zeist 1927.
H. Kohl und C. Watzinger. Antike Synagogen in Galilea, Leipzig 1916.
A. Köster. Das antike Seewesen, Berlin 1923.
R. A. S. Macalister. A Century of Excavation in Palestine, London.
F. W. Madden. History of the Jewish Coinage and of Money in the Old and
  New Testament, London 1864.
G. P. Marang. Bijbelsche en Oud-Joodsche Munten, Nijkerk 1919.
Otis Tufton Mason. Primitive Travel and Transportation (Report of the
  U.S. National Museum), Washington 1896.
B. Meissner. Babylonien und Assyrien I, II, Heidelberg 1920, 1925.
M. S. Miller and J. Lane Miller. Encyclopedia of Bible Life.
A. Musil. Arabia Petraea I–III, Wien 1907, 1908.
James Neil. Everyday Life in the Holy Land, 1924.
A. Noordtzij. Gods Woord en der eeuwen getuigenis, Kampen 1931.
A. Noordtzij. Palestina en het land van den Jordaan, Ludwig Preiss.
M. Noth. Die Welt des Alten Testaments, Berlin 1940.
H. Th. Obbink. Oostersch leven, I, II, Nijkerk 1914, 1915.
H. Perdrizet. Le monument de Hermel, Syria 1938.
J. van der Ploeg, O.P. Jaarbericht "Ex Oriente Lux" No. 11.
A. Racinet. Le costume historique I, Paris.
C. Rathjens und H. v. Wissmann. Landeskundliche Ergebnisse (Südarabien
  Reise.) Hamburg University; Band 40; 1934.
A. Reifenberg. Ancient Hebrew Arts.
W. Reimpell. Geschichte der babylonischen und assyrischen Kleidung,
  Berlin 1921.
A. Rowe and L. H. Vincent. New Light on the Evolution of Canaanite
  Temples as Exemplified by Restorations of the Sanctuaries Found at
  Beth-Shan. Palestine Exploration Fund. 1931.
C. Sächs. Altägyptische Musikinstrumente, Leipzig 1920.
C. Schick. Artuf und seine Umgebung. Zeitschr. des deutschen Palästina
  Vereins 1887.
C. Schick. Die Stiftshütte, der Tempel in Jerusalem und der Tempelplatz der
  Jetztzeit, Berlin 1896.
Frank Scholten. Palestine Illustrated (two volumes).
Rev. L. Schouten Hzn. De Tabernakel, Gods heiligdom bij Israël, Utrecht 1887.
J. Simons, S.J. Opgravingen in Palestina, Roermond-Maaseik (1935).
J. Simons, S.J. Twee nieuw-gevonden zegels uit het Bijbelsche Lachish.
  Studiën, Juli 1941.
I. Snoek. De Handelingen der Apostelen, Rotterdam 1933.
I. Snoek. Koningen van Israëls God gegeven, Kampen 1938.
I. Snoek. In Bethlehem en in Nazareth, Rotterdam 1938.
Merrill F. Unger. Archaeology and the Old Testament, 1957.
Merrill F. Unger. Unger's Bible Dictionary, 1957.
R. de Vaux, O.P. La grotte des manuscrits Hébreux. Revue Biblique LVI.
P. Hugues Vincent. Canaan d'après l'exploration recente, Paris 1907.
L. H. Vincent, O.P. Les fouilles de Byblos. Revue Biblique XXXIV; 1925.

BIBLIOGRAPHY

L. H. Vincent, O.P. L'Antonia et le Prétoire. Revue Biblique **XLII**; 1933.
J. Th. de Visser. Hebreeuwse Archeologie, Utrecht.
J. G. Wilkinson—S. Birch. The Manners and Customs of the Ancient Egyptians, London 1878.
C. Watzinger. Denkmäler Palästinas, I, II, Leipzig 1933, 1935.
J. D. Whiting. Canoeing Down the River Jordan. The National Geographic Magazine, 1940.
C. L. Woolley. Ur und die Sintflut, Leipzig 1931.